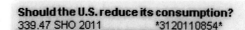

At Issue

Should the U.S. Reduce Its Consumption?

Other Books in the At Issue Series:

At Issue

Should the U.S. Reduce Its Consumption?

David Haugen and Susan Musser, Book Editors

GREENHAVEN PRESS
A part of Gale, Cengage Learning

GALE
CENGAGE Learning·

Detroit • New York • San Francisco • New Haven, Conn • Waterville, Maine • London

Christine Nasso, *Publisher*
Elizabeth Des Chenes, *Managing Editor*

© 2011 Greenhaven Press, a part of Gale, Cengage Learning.

Gale and Greenhaven Press are registered trademarks used herein under license.

For more information, contact:
Greenhaven Press
27500 Drake Rd.
Farmington Hills, MI 48331-3535
Or you can visit our Internet site at gale.cengage.com

For product information and technology assistance, contact us at

Gale Customer Support, 1-800-877-4253
For permission to use material from this text or product, submit all requests online at www.cengage.com/permissions

Further permissions questions can be emailed to permissionrequest@cengage.com

Articles in Greenhaven Press anthologies are often edited for length to meet page requirements. In addition, original titles of these works are changed to clearly present the main thesis and to explicitly indicate the author's opinion. Every effort is made to ensure that Greenhaven Press accurately reflects the original intent of the authors. Every effort has been made to trace the owners of copyrighted material.

Cover image copyright © Images.com/Corbis.

LIBRARY OF CONGRESS CATALOGING-IN-PUBLICATION DATA

Should the U.S. reduce its consumption? / David Haugen and Susan Musser, book editors.
       p. cm. -- (At issue)
   Includes bibliographical references and index.
   ISBN 978-0-7377-4894-9 (hbk.) -- ISBN 978-0-7377-4895-6 (pbk.)
   1. Consumption (Economics)--United States--Juvenile literature. 2. Consumers--United States--Juvenile literature. I. Haugen, David M., 1969- II. Musser, Susan.
   HC110.C6S54 2010
   339.4'70973--dc22
                                                        2010020771

Printed in the United States of America
1 2 3 4 5 6 7 14 13 12 11 10

Contents

Introduction

The financial crisis that struck across the globe in 2008 forced many Americans to reconsider their spending habits. According to a November 5, 2008, Reuters news report, purchases of furniture, electronics, appliances, and other items exceeding $1,000 in value dropped off dramatically. Other areas of consumer luxury spending also slowed in the early stages of the crisis. Quoting the retail tracking service SpendingPulse, Reuters reported, "October specialty apparel sales fell 12.2 percent from a year earlier. Women's apparel sales dropped 18.2 percent, while men's apparel sales fell 8.3 percent. Footwear sales dropped 9.7 percent." Faced with rising gas prices and high food costs, Americans slashed their spending on nonessential goods enough to cause retailers to worry. A year later, the news was still fairly dire for stores and other vendors. In an October 12, 2009, issue of *The New Yorker*, financial page staff writer James Surowiecki concluded, "This recession has permanently remade American consumers, turning them from spendthrifts into tightwads." Yet Surowiecki was unsure that the financial downturn was encouraging a new mindset among U.S. consumers. He simply noted that "Americans have been spending less because they have less money to spend."

Surowiecki remained skeptical that the new thriftiness would last. He pointed out that just after the belt-tightening that characterized the Great Depression of the 1930s, Americans readily resumed spending on luxury items in the 1940s and 1950s. Surowiecki commented, "If the Depression didn't make Americans wary of the pleasures of consumption, it's unlikely that this downturn will." Other analysts are not so sure. Writing on the Naked Capitalism Web site, Edward Harrison of Credit Writedowns, a top financial blog, claimed on August 16, 2008, that consumer spending would likely remain weak for years as Americans struggle to pay down the huge personal debts they acquired in the years before the financial meltdown. "It's hard to spend more when you have a mountain of debt staring you in the face," Harrison observed. Other experts point to high levels of job loss across the economy as a factor that will presumably keep spending down.

The debate over spending patterns during the recession, though, has prompted a much larger discussion in the country. Many Americans are wondering if the current crisis might serve as a lesson that the nation can no longer support rampant consumerism. Some contend that living in a consumerist nation has lured people into debt and made them dissatisfied with the numerous possessions they own. Writing in the *Ecologist* in March 2009, writer and corporate advisor Jules Peck states that "people who live their lives framed around extrinsic values of self-focus, image, greed and acquisition, and are suffering from 'affluenza', are diminishing their own wellbeing as well as those around them." He believes that emphasizing intrinsic values and self-growth is the way to derail overspending and revamp the culture. Reporting for the *New York Times* on April 12, 2008, Ed Bark shifts the focus away from personal wellbeing to national and even global wellbeing. Speaking of the "human footprint" evaluation measured by the National Geographic Society, Bark writes, "Americans continue to out-big-foot everyone else when it comes to consumption. Although only 5 percent of the global population, Americans are said to use more than one-quarter of the world's energy." In contrast, a healthy "human footprint" is achieved through a balance of consumption and need. Americans, however, use far more resources than they need to live sustainably.

The problem, as many analysts claim, is not only about consuming more resources but also about producing more pollution as an end result of that consumption. As the National Geographic *Human Footprint* educational resource pamphlet claims, "By their first birthday, the average American will be responsible for more carbon dioxide emissions than a person in Tanzania generates in a lifetime." This level of emissions is due only slightly to the gasoline used in transporting an American child from place to place. The majority of those emissions stem from energy used to heat the child's home, gasoline used to transport baby food across the country (even across the globe) to local supermarkets, the energy used in manufacturing and shipping the hundreds of disposable diapers to local retailers, and a host of other hidden energy expenditures that place baby products and services within reach of the child's parents. A person living in a developing nation like Tanzania simply does not have access to such conveniences. Autos and disposable diapers might be an unaffordable luxury, and people in developing parts of the world tend to buy food that is grown and sold locally. Their human footprint is, by comparison, much smaller.

On August 9, 2008, an ABC News poll recorded that 7 in 10 Americans say they are trying to reduce their energy, or carbon, footprint by driving less and opting for smaller and more fuel-efficient cars and by reducing home energy and water use. Although 25 percent claimed they were adopting these measures to save money in the faltering economy, 33 percent insisted they were cutting down their carbon footprint to help the environment. Still, among those Americans who reported that they were not reducing energy consumption, 54 percent said that "it's unnecessary, too expensive, too inconvenient, won't do any good, or that they just aren't interested." Clearly, though, this sector of the population is in the minority, according to the poll, suggesting that the message of reducing waste is reaching most Americans.

Indeed, some assert that Americans are not the over-consumers that the media makes them out to be. Harvard law professor Elizabeth Warren has argued for several years that the portrait of Americans as spendthrifts is undermined by spending statistics. According to Warren, middle-income

Americans in the twenty-first century spend less on luxury goods, clothing, groceries, and appliances than they did in the 1970s. Present-day Americans saw the most drastic increases in spending over their counterparts in the 1970s, Warren says, in necessities. "On housing, they were spending more than 100 percent more," Warren stated in a February 19, 2010, Fox News video. "Same thing on health insurance; same thing on child care because now they have two people in the workforce; same thing on transportation because now they have to have two cars in order to get somebody to work; and spending more on taxes." While Warren does not dispute that most Americans are in debt because they consumed more than they could afford, she maintains the expenditures were not for frivolous luxuries but for services they could not afford to do without, and some of these—like healthcare, child care, and taxes—the modern consumer has no recourse but to pay what is demanded.

In *At Issue: Should the U.S. Reduce Its Consumption?* experts, reporters, and pundits from various backgrounds address the question of whether America should change its consumption habits. Some contend that every citizen has to learn to consume fewer resources and live within their means; others insist that Americans are already cutting expenses and consumption and that overzealousness may be wrongheaded. Regardless, many Americans feel they hoard and store more things than they need, and large numbers of them have striven to simplify their lives not only to reduce consumption but to reduce clutter. Only time will tell whether a commitment to this new philosophy will benefit individuals and help the planet. After all, thrift has chiefly been forced on Americans during lean times, and skeptics remain unconvinced that America can ultimately be anything other than a consumerist nation.

1

The U.S. Is a Consumer Nation

Tirdad Derakhshani

Tirdad Derakhshani teaches film studies, philosophy, and religion courses at Penn State University. He is also a staff writer for the Philadelphia Inquirer.

Whereas once America's economic health was measured by how much its citizens produced and saved, today consumption has become the yardstick. Modern American consumers spend to make themselves feel better, believing their habits are powering the nation's economy. Advertising supports this notion, enticing Americans to define themselves by what they buy and encouraging them to think that all comforts and goods are within reach. Unfortunately, the pleasure derived from consumerism is only temporary, and eventually the nation will recognize that such rampant spending cannot go on indefinitely.

A Black Friday mob of frenzied shoppers breaks down the doors of a Walmart on Long Island, N.Y., and tramples an employee to death. Four others are injured, including a woman who is eight months pregnant.

Most of those condemning the incident treat it as an aberration, a display of craven greed in an otherwise healthy community. One commentator even blamed the tragedy on the severe pressures and anxieties caused by the economic meltdown.

Perhaps it would be more fruitful to treat it as a symbol of a fanatical, hyperconsumerist ethos, which has come to define us as individuals and as a community.

Trampling incidents evoke images of mindless crowds whipped into a frenzy by an ideology that arouses an uncontrollable, irrational desire.

If there's an antidote to such an ideology, surely it's consumerism, which promises individual freedom, autonomy and rational choice. Yet at its extreme, consumerism creates the same fanatical crowd behavior that has led to trampling deaths at rock concerts, European soccer games, and the annual hajj in Saudi Arabia.

Sadly, hundreds were trampled at the hajj between 1987 and 2004. Those deaths are used by some Westerners as proof that Islam engenders a mob mentality and destroys individual autonomy.

Consumerism, no less than any cult or religion, has the power to level individual difference and independence and render citizens into a homogeneous mass. Advertising companies, celebrity spokespersons, movies and TV shows conspire to render the consumer object—be it a $2 ice cream cone or an $80,000 luxury sedan—into a fetish imbued with magical, if not downright divine, powers. (Consumerism also has its rituals and its holy days, most notably Black Friday itself.)

Today, the country's economic health is measured more according to how much we are willing to spend, our consumer confidence, and less in how much we produce, the gross national product, or even how we invest.

If this sounds excessive, think of the frenzied desire someone like Michael Jackson, Paul McCartney, Britney Spears or Allen Iverson has evoked in otherwise rational people. The primitive, visceral reaction we feel as fans is the same infantile desire aroused by consumer goods.

The consumerist message has become the wallpaper to our lives.

"Enjoy," flashes a billboard-size red neon Coke sign. Enjoy [COCA-COLA] . . . Enjoy [COCA-COLA] . . . Enjoy . . . This is not merely a cheerful suggestion. It's a command.

In the 21st century, pleasure is equated to consumption, and consumption has become an imperative that has all but replaced the moral imperative issued by teachers from Abraham to 18th-century philosopher Immanuel Kant and 20th-century liberators Gandhi and the Rev. Dr. Martin Luther King Jr.

The old moral tradition gave birth to our grandparents' credo, the so-called Protestant work ethic—work hard, sacrifice, and invest wisely in the future.

Today, the country's economic health is measured more according to how much we are willing to spend, our consumer confidence, and less in how much we produce, the gross national product, or even how we invest.

If previous leaders preached self-sacrifice and service, our commander in chief tells us that our duty is to consume. Since Sept. 11, he has consistently told Americans that if we want to help the country, we must . . . buy.

To be American once meant having the right to pursue happiness, where the emphasis is on the road taken toward a goal that is difficult, if not impossible, to teach—at least in one lifetime. Today our right is to be happy. (Enjoy . . . enjoy . . . enjoy.)

Consumerism infantilizes us, alienates us from one another, and makes us apathetic as citizens. What's ironic is that even if you base human worth not on social responsibility but on individual happiness, consumerism still fails us.

A consumer economy only works if consumption of goods provides only temporary pleasure. That is, if happiness is infinitely deferred, so that buyers continue to buy more and more goods and services. By definition, the consumer can never be satisfied, at rest or happy. Which means she will always feel lacking. The pursuit of this sort of happiness creates a vicious circle of growing anxiety and dissatisfaction.

Perhaps what's most dismaying is that so many consumers have become sophisticated enough to know they are manipulated, yet choose to remain passive.

We are like the 30-something characters in *Seinfeld*, who know they are immature, who know they are avoiding the responsibility of building meaningful relationships and of leading meaningful lives—and who don't really care.

The reason is simple: We are, for the most part, comfortable.

But, given the global economic crisis and the rapid rate at which we are consuming Earth's resources, how long can our little comforts last?

2

The U.S. Is a Producer Nation

Richard M. Abrams

Richard M. Abrams is a professor of the Graduate School in the Department of History at the University of California-Berkeley. He is the author of America Transformed: Sixty Years of Revolutionary Change, 1941–2001.

America has always been fixated on its ability to produce goods. Production drives the economy, and the government recognizes this fact. For this reason, producers, not consumers, have benefited the most from laws and public policies. The government and the courts commonly ignore or overrule the rights of consumers when the capacity of America's production—and thus the health of the economy—is threatened. Oddly, consumers have accepted this second-class status; their willingness to sacrifice their rights probably stems from their belief that they are part of the big production machine, driving the economy and making the nation stronger.

A blooming industry among pundits, journalists, historians, and others celebrates, although more often deplores, America as "a consumer society." One prize-winning historian [Lizabeth Cohen] has described the country as "A Consumer's Republic," suggesting that consumers own the place. Another [Timothy Breen] argues how consumers "shaped" American politics even from the very beginning of the nation in the eighteenth century. Still another [Meg Jacobs] argues that it was consumer interests that "fueled liberal politics" from at least the beginning of the twentieth century. Not everyone agrees on what is meant by the term. But the elements of the idea include the importance of consumer goods for recreation, for creature comforts, for self-esteem, for social standing, for the country's prosperity, and in general for Americans' access to affluence.

But can "consumer society" also accurately describe the American polity? I think not.

A Nation Defined by Production

To characterize the United States as "a consumer society" at any time in its history misdirects attention from its most important and persistent trait. Whether the economy is fueled by Americans' avid shopping for consumer goods or by industry's consumption of capital goods, the focus of the economy *and of public policy* in America has remained on *production*. For a few years in the late 1960s and early 1970s, there was a surge of national legislation designed by and for consumer interests. Except for that brief window, American politics has turned almost exclusively on the competition for government favor among rival claims for the rewards of production. For businesses and employers, that meant tax exemptions, depletion allowances, infrastructure development, legal and police restraints on labor agitation and unions, protective tariffs to insure profits, direct subsidies to selected industries, assistance in promoting exports, tort reform, and various other profit-generating incentives. For labor, it meant support for improving wages and working conditions, social insurance, immigration restrictions, protective tariffs to ensure jobs, and collective bargaining rights. For farmers it also meant (different) tariff walls, special access to foreign workers during harvest season, government protection against the spread of agricultural pests and disease, subsidies for crop-improvement research, as well as direct subsidies to boost commodity prices and, indeed, to pad the incomes of certain farmers and agribusinesses.

The Food and Drugs and the Meat Inspection Acts of the Progressive Era [1890s to 1920s] might seem to be exceptions. But in fact they are not. When Upton Sinclair wrote *The Jungle*, about the meatpacking industry, his focus was on working conditions—the conditions under which the *producers* labored. And although consumers must have responded as consumers to reports of contaminated meats, what pushed the legislation through was the pressure from Swift, Armour, Cudahy, and other big packers. They needed the government's imprimatur to overcome the foreign embargoes against their export business that followed from the turn-of-the-century scandals about spoilage, contamination, and adulteration—a problem created mostly by small packers who needed to cut corners to survive in competition with the biggies. The same was true of the Federal Drug Administration [FDA], where honest-to-goodness pharmaceutical companies needed to overcome the popularity (among consumers) of the snake-oil hucksters and [nineteenth-century marketer] Lydia Pinkham's highly successful patent medicine [that claimed to relieve menstrual and menopausal symptoms]. These were producers' triumphs, not consumer victories, however much consumers may have benefited as the result of the contest for advantage among competing sectors of an industry.

For only about . . . five years or so at the end of the third quarter of the twentieth century were federal and some state laws and regulations passed to protect consumers against flawed and dangerous products.

What about the Sherman Anti-Trust Act? A consumer victory? Not so. U.S. antitrust policy originated primarily in an effort to protect competitors rather than consumers; to stop the "trusts" from "denying the rights of the common man in business," as one congressman put it in 1900. According to prevailing theory, a competitive multitude among producers not only checked the concentration of power in the country but, equally important, served to build individual character upon which the success of a self-governing people vitally depended. "Only through the participation by the many in the responsibilities and determinations of business," wrote Justice Louis Brandeis in *Liggett v. Lee,* an early-twentieth-century antitrust case, "can Americans secure the moral and intellectual development essential to the maintenance of liberty."

[Congress has rejected] proposals to elevate a Consumer Protection Administration to cabinet level, alongside the producer-promoting departments of Agriculture, Labor, and Commerce.

The nation's political history simply does not support the notion of America as "a consumer society." For only about the previously mentioned five years or so at the end of the third quarter of the twentieth century were federal and some state laws and regulations passed to protect consumers against flawed and dangerous products. Only then were manufacturers required to inform consumers with some precision just what it was that they would soon put in their house or in their mouth. Only then would producers be required to print on their packages the true ingredients of products and their net weights and to provide information about ingredients such as peanut or sesame oil that could activate fatal allergic reactions in some consumers. Only then did public policy transfer back to producers, at least partially, the external costs of production that for more than a century the society at large had absorbed in the form of ailments and injuries arising from hazardous product ingredients, hazardous working conditions, and polluted soil, air, and water.

It took a series of scandals to bring consumer interests to the attention of American politics. The thalidomide disaster of 1961–1962 called attention to the FDA's poor servicing of consumers' interest in safe pharmaceuticals. The work of [consumer advocate] Ralph Nader early in the sixties projected a spotlight on corporate arrogance by exposing the attempt by General Motors to cover up the flawed design of the company's subcompact, Corvair, which had a lamentable tendency to flip over when making sharp turns.

Production Wins Out in Court and in the Legislature

But the brief enthusiasm for consumer interests soon dissipated. By 1975, government policies had reverted to their almost exclusive emphasis on producers' concerns. As the deregulation movement got under way, new transgressions against consumers gained little attention. Ford management memoranda revealed that the company had coldly calculated that to recall its Pinto model, because the gasoline tank was dangerously situated, would be more expensive than to pay off the many victims of incendiary crashes (at an officially estimated cost of $200,000 per human life). There was no recall. The state of Illinois lost a criminal case against the company because it was determined that the government's "risk/benefit" formula, designed to encourage "economic efficiency," protected producers from liability when the cost of minimizing the risks to human safety exceeded the anticipated social benefits.

Congress and the American people continued to make clear their overwhelming preference for producer interests over consumer interests. Early in the decade, the government permitted the railroad companies to cut passenger service, thereby making it more difficult for people to travel and helping to clog the highways with automobiles. Even today, many states require passenger trains to yield the right of way to freight trains, further discouraging rail travel by greatly lengthening intercity trips.

In 1977, Congress defeated a measure to require used-car dealers to reveal to customers what might be wrong with the heaps they were hawking. The nation's representatives followed that up by rejecting proposals to elevate a Consumer Protection Administration to cabinet level, alongside the producer-promoting departments of Agriculture, Labor, and Commerce.

Producers' Rights Remain Paramount in Public Policy

In the 1980s, despite a decades-long-delayed court ruling that the Federal Communications Commission [FCC] had to permit consumer interests to present their views to the commission at hearings on the distribution of radio and television frequencies, the FCC, with the tacit approval of Congress, persisted in giving its attention solely to producer groups. Only industry members continued to have meaningful access to the FCC, to the exclusion of consumers' concerns for quality, educational, or public interest programming. At the same time, the public's interest in access to political information took a backseat to the media corporations' "free speech" rights, when the courts ruled that the FCC could not require radio and television stations—increasingly controlled by a dwindling handful of megacorporate managers—to permit rebuttals to editorials and programs that promoted particular political, social, or religious causes. Consumers' interest in a balanced, authoritative presentation of information—the crucial ingredient of "rational choice" in a market-oriented polity—was the distinct loser.

Producer lobbying—and that includes farmers, union workers, processors, and manufacturers—continued to frustrate the efforts of consumer groups and even foreign governments to require U.S. food marketers to properly label goods that contained ingredients that had undergone hormone or gene-altering treatment. There may be nothing wrong with the use of hormones or with gene-engineering for foods, but one might believe that consumers should have the right to know about them. Nor were efforts successful to require producers and distributors of many fresh food products to specify the country or state of origin.

[Many] judicial decisions . . . make it impossible to impose significant penalties on producers even after they are found guilty of having lied over decades about the dangers of their products.

With the advent of George W. Bush's presidency, the reactionary drift became a landslide. Consumer interests were deliberately excluded from policymaking, whether in the shaping of energy policy, conserving open space, wetlands, and wilderness areas, controlling climate-changing and toxic industrial and vehicular emissions, or restraining monopoly power among producer firms, especially in the media, energy, and financial sectors. Pro-producer measures during the administration of George the Second would reach what many people once considered to be unimaginable levels. In 2005, for example, the agriculture department *prohibited* cattle ranchers from testing their own animals for Creutzfeldt-Jakob (mad cow) disease, because such testing might give consumers information that could injure the industry. The FDA refused to require pharmaceutical companies to make public the outcome of their own tests on their old and new products, although some of those secret tests turned up dangerous side effects. Inevitably, there arose scandals of cover-ups once individual tragedies came to light. In 2006, government agencies withheld information for several days about an E. coli outbreak traceable to domestic spinach on the grounds that such information might "panic" consumers and injure producers. Consumers' access to information that could affect their health was blocked because of producers' higher interests.

In 2003, Bush proposed eliminating or reducing to insignificance the income tax as the main source of government revenues, substituting instead a *tax on consumption*. The country had long been gravitating toward a revenue system that relied heavily on sales and excise taxes, and most particularly on user fees (tuition, tolls, licenses, permits, admission fees for museums, public gardens, and zoos, as well as parking fees at hiking trailheads, park picnic sites, and metro stations), all burdens imposed directly on consumers.

Then there are the judicial decisions that make it impossible to impose significant penalties on producers even after they are found guilty of having lied over decades about the dangers of their products. In August 2006, a federal judge ruled that the cigarette companies charged with violating racketeering laws had systematically deceived the public for five decades about the dangers of tobacco. The companies' executives knew all that time that the products that they aggressively sold to the public had toxic and potentially fatal ingredients, while they publicly lied (at one time, under oath before a congressional committee) about the safety of their products. But, the judge said, she did not have the authority to order significant financial remedies. Why? Because an industry-friendly appellate court had ruled earlier that sanctions against the law violators must be "forward looking," meaning the courts could not impose substantial fines for past crimes but essentially could only order a change in the industry's future behavior. *The Wall Street Journal* remarked, "For most companies a finding from a federal judge that they were racketeers would be a stinging blow," but "their efforts to hide the risks of smoking are well known," and so there was no reason to expect that their already tarnished image would suffer any further. The ruling produced an immediate surge in the price of tobacco company securities. A producer-friendly appellate court earlier had also ruled that the government could not seek to recover from the industry the public's costs in treating Americans whose health suffered from the fraud perpetrated over the decades by the companies.

Everyday Burdens Placed on Consumers

But the priority of producer over consumer interests should not require revelations from the media. It is obvious to anyone with eyes to see and bodies to be comforted. Contemplate the design of most airplanes and airports and explain how high consumer/user interests rank in the society's priorities. Enter an airport and sit, sometimes for hours, with a thousand other consumers of airline services in a stifling waiting room with a twelve-foot ceiling; or wedge yourself into a fifteen-by-eighteen-inch seat, where your neighbor's backrest protrudes within a foot of your chest; or stand anxiously by one of the four or five toilets provided onboard to serve four hundred passengers and try to imagine how lucky you are to live in "a consumer society." Nor do the rules seem consumer-friendly that allow overbooked airlines to bump passengers waiting to board; or to deny a passenger the right to switch to another airline without further charges when various troubles on the booked airline lead to many hours of delay, and sometimes cause cancellation too late for a passenger to find a reasonable alternative mode of travel—to say nothing of the costs of missing a connecting flight.

How consumer friendly are those gas stations (once called service stations) that require consumers to pump their own gas or else pay an outsize premium per gallon? And can there be more frustrating moments in a working day than fighting with an electronic "pay station" in parking garages and lots that employ no attendants at all ("cost savings") and where the often balky machine must produce an entry ticket; and then later process the parking slip to permit exiting?

How are consumer interests served when personal telephone records are legally available for a price and for sale at a profit? (Locatecell.com is only one corporation that legally mines and then sells such information to any business or government agency that cares to pay for it.) Consumers of cellphone services come last when producers see profit opportunities. The same applies to the records kept by department stores, brokerage houses, banks, and insurance companies whose "privacy" notices explain how their clientele have in fact no privacy rights whatever. (Read the fine print.) Nor are personal medical records exempted from the profiteering work of data miners. (Try the Medical Information Bureau.)

Consumers are themselves to blame, seeing themselves first as producers rather than consumers.

Consumers Are Not Complaining

How well are consumer interests served when the law allows pushers of products to intrude at will upon our telephones, Internet, and fax machines? Or to pop ads onto television screens, more or less continuously, during an ongoing drama, sitcom, or sports program; or onto a computer screen, sometimes freezing a word-processing session? Can one rent a DVD anymore without having to endure multiple ads for other films before being permitted to see the film rented? To say nothing of the fifteen or twenty minutes of both film and product advertising forced on moviegoers before the film they have paid for appears on the screen. Even national public radio and television stations, partly supported by consumer subscriptions, now present several minutes of ads each hour, necessitated by cuts in congressional support. More than eighty years ago, that old radical Herbert Hoover, then secretary of commerce when radio was new, declared. "It is unconceivable that we should allow so great a possibility for service to be drowned in advertising." How quaint!

Consumers are themselves to blame, seeing themselves first as producers rather than consumers. If there are many who would complain, the media—which are dependent on producers' ads—are not likely to give them much time or space. But who's complaining?

If America has become truly "a consumer society," its politics and policies hardly reflect it. It would be much more accurate to speak of "consumerism" as a producer's target; or even as a producer's invention. Of course, "All producers are also consumers; and probably most consumers are also producers." But it is the capacity in which people conceive of themselves that drives policy. And if it is at all possible to infer that public policy reflects public desires, then we must deduce that for all the centrality of consumer goods for the maintenance of a prosperous economy, for bolstering self-respect, for satisfying recreational desires, and for making claims to social standing, Americans still think of themselves first and above all as producers rather than as consumers.

3

The U.S. Must Rethink Its Consumption Habits

Ted Anthony

Ted Anthony is an assistant managing editor at Associated Press.
His journalism has focused on American culture.

Americans are ravenous consumers, outspending their incomes
and hoping that their credit will allow them to purchase all the
latest conveniences and luxuries. The 2008 financial crisis was a
wake-up call for overextended Americans. Some began saving
and cutting back on extraneous purchases, but it is still unclear
whether America as a whole has embraced thrift. In the past,
U.S. presidents encouraged frugality and the Great Depression
taught people the value of their money, but in more modern
times the message has changed, and presidents and advertisers
have prompted Americans to pump more money into the
economy. Only time will tell if the lessons of the current recession
will persuade citizens to take fiscal responsibility and balance
saving with spending.

The first thing you see is the enormous boot.

Atop a ridge north of Pittsburgh, towering over customers at the entrance to Ross Park Mall, the giant L.L. Bean boot seems to shout: No buy is too big, no shopping dream too outsized. Come on in. Retail nirvana awaits. "Please do not climb on the boot," says a sign, as if we all might.

Ted Anthony, "Slapped by Recession, Can Consumer Nation Rethink?" FoxNews.com,
March 21, 2009. Reprinted with permission of the Associated Press.

Inside, along buffed corridors freshly retooled to ramp up the aura of luxury, storefront signs spin a tale of a culture in conflict. "More choices coming soon," says a store under construction. "Unmounted Diamond Event," trumpets Littman Jewelers.

Yet selected items at Ann Taylor and Morini are 60 percent off. Le Gourmet Chef exhorts everyone to "Buy More $ave More"—a truth and a paradox that distills America into a bumper-sticker slogan. And just past the front door is the place that touts "Great Deals Inside." That would be Citizens Bank.

Credit—personal and institutional and national—is overextended into the absurd.

These are the contradictions that confront 21st-century America. We love to shop, but we need to save. We want it all, and we want it now. No matter whether it's a new pair of $100 jeans on your Visa, 90 days same as cash on that new car, a subprime mortgage. Psychologically, they're of a piece: Buy now, pay later. Shop 'til you drop.

Now we're paying. Now we're dropping. Credit—personal and institutional and national—is overextended into the absurd. Money that didn't exist in the first place is now frighteningly, heartbreakingly real. And the temples of our consumer choice are starting to crumble.

Chrysler and General Motors are wondering aloud if their century-old tanks are empty. Starbucks, home of the $4 venti latte, is laying off thousands and has—et tu, Brute?—launched a cheap brand of instant coffee. Circuit City expired two weeks ago, leaving 567 stores dark and Best Buy as the main place to shop for the 60-inch flat-screen HDTV you can't afford.

This is economic crisis. And in Washington and on Wall Street, they're scrambling to fix it with economic cures—useful ones or misguided ones, depending upon your perspective. But however effective they are, they remain attempts to impose a financial solution upon a dilemma that, in many ways, is cultural and behavioral.

Because in America, we consume. It is what we do, what we have been told to do, what our government usually tells us to do, what we love to do and what we must do. It has built us into a behemoth and undercut us at inopportune moments. Viewed from a distance, it's easy to see us as a nation of economic 5-year-olds, spending our allowance before we get it and demanding more, more, more, then being shocked when the money runs out.

Well, our revels now are ended. And at the edges of any economic recovery that might lie ahead lurks a question that few seem inclined to contemplate: At the dawn of the administration that swore it would bring change to us, can we bring change to ourselves?

The conundrum of America has long been thus—thrift and parsimony vs. capitalism and acquisition.

The Jan. 29 White House daily briefing offered a telling moment when the question of what to do with federal stimulus money came up. "The point of an economic stimulus plan," presidential press secretary Robert Gibbs said, "is to get money into people's hands and into people's pockets so that they use their hand to reach in their pocket and spend that money."

But wait, someone said. Hold on. What about savings? Wasn't it the nationwide lack of savings and overextension of credit—institutional and personal—that got us into this mess? Gibbs was quick and emphatic: "I'm not discouraging savings," he said.

And therein lies the tension. It's like the old Warner Bros. cartoons in which Daffy Duck or some other character has miniature versions of himself on his shoulder—one a gentle angel, the other a pitchfork-wielding devil—giving him polar opposite accounts of what to do next. Shop? Save? Shop more?

The conundrum of America has long been thus—thrift and parsimony vs. capitalism and acquisition. Both are virtues. One is seen as small-town and heartland, and thus appealing. The other, on an institutional level, elevated America into an economic giant and, on a personal level, made us a nation of debtors with really cool toys and houses we can't pay for.

They can seem irreconcilable. Even as Calvin Coolidge was cautioning that "thrift and self-control are not sought because they create wealth, but because they create character," John Maynard Keynes was insisting that "the engine which drives enterprise is not thrift, but profit."

When bad things happen, the instinct is to batten the hatches and not spend. That's why George W. Bush had to tell us to get out and shop after 9/11. As absurd as it sounded, the message was solid: Don't quit the economy or it will quit you.

But the genius of America has always been its penchant for believing in better days ahead, not worse ones, so it's difficult to justify saving for a rainy day when the national narrative expects sunny skies. That's why about the only thing that made sense in Jim Cramer's comments to Jon Stewart earlier this month was when he said that of course he thought the market would keep going up; hadn't it been doing so for years?

Is it any wonder we're confused?

Amid the encouragement to buy, encouragements to save—truly save rather than just buy one and get one free—are emerging.

Slowly, though, signs are emerging that suggest the recent months of economic free fall and attendant angst have gotten our attention. Luxury shopping—goods bought at places like

Coach and Neiman Marcus—was down 19.2 percent in February from a year ago, according to the International Council of Shopping Centers. And an AP/GfK poll last month showed that 65 percent of Americans questioned worried about whether they'd be able to pay their bills.

"Mentally, it's already changing. We always wondered, what were they like, those people of the Great Depression—how did they learn how to save? And now we're becoming like them," says Amity Shlaes, author of "The Forgotten Man: A New History of the Great Depression."

Amid the encouragement to buy, encouragements to save—truly save rather than just buy one and get one free—are emerging.

Feedthepig.org, a savings advice site, enlists a straight-talking pig in a pink suit named Benjamin—alarming but effective—to encourage young adults from 25 to 34 to stick coins into the slot in his head. Its Web traffic soared by almost 40,000 in January as the recession deepened. Its all-ages counterpart, 360financialliteracy.org, which doesn't use talking ham, breaks down financial common sense into life stages with a depth and breadth that would make Ben Franklin's penny-saved heart soar.

What's particularly interesting about these initiatives is who's behind them: the professional organization for American accountants, AICPA, whose leaders were alarmed when they learned three years ago that the national savings rate was a negative figure for the first time since the Depression.

"As a nation, economically, I think we got very soft. It just got too easy," says Carl George, CEO of the Illinois accounting firm Clifton Gunderson and chairman of the National CPA Financial Literacy Commission.

"The message has been let's revitalize or make the economy more vital, and the way to do that is to insert your own personal capital into the economy," George says. "And I think, 'OK, that's a good message IF you can afford it.' But you know

what? If you can't afford to go out and buy that widescreen
. . . you haven't done anybody any good."

Americans are not known for being introspective, but rage
at the Bernard Madoffs of the world may be encouraging even
that. People look at the CEOs and the big-bank bailouts and
the private jets, and suddenly Gordon Gekko saying "Greed is
good" doesn't sound all that cinematic anymore.

Lydia Perez-Carpenter, an actress and waitress in New
York, sees some of that. At 25, she has seen many friends in
recent months "finding the cheap way of doing what we want
to do" or, even, contemplating savings and frugality. She has
put a rubber band around her credit card to remind herself
that it's money she doesn't have.

"Most of my generation has this concept that, 'Oh, I'll just
put it on my credit card.' Then we're sitting here paying hundreds of dollars a month on credit-card debt, and it'll never
go away," she says. "We definitely need an attitude adjustment.
The American way of thinking in my mind is wanting whatever we want now with very little long term-thinking. Hope-
fully that's changing."

Wishful thinking, but perhaps realism's moment is at hand.
Can it be we didn't realize that our instant-gratification culture ran so deep that it permeated not only our wallets and
our attitudes but our financial institutions as well? Can it further be that the vaunted indicator of "consumer confidence" is
a double-edged sword, and that buying—pardon, "infusing
money into the economy"—isn't the best starting point from
which to view our lot?

Tod Porter, who heads the economics department at
Youngstown State University in Ohio, one of the country's
most struggling areas, sees us struggling through the cloudy
waters of what economists call "the paradox of thrift." In this
model, savings operates like a daily multivitamin. In sensible
doses it is a virtue that fosters stability and keeps the system

strong. But in excess, it can be poisonous to the system by reducing the demand for goods and services—and making bad recessions worse.

For the moment, though, we are reaping the aftereffects of not taking our vitamins. The system is broken, and many of the vandals are, in fact, us.

Can it be we didn't realize that our instant-gratification culture ran so deep that it permeated not only our wallets and our attitudes but our financial institutions as well?

"It was like Wile E. Coyote running off the cliff, and for a while he doesn't realize there's nothing underneath him. And that can only last so long," Porter says. His voice trails off, and he poses a question.

"At what point does everybody realize the game is up?"

So can we change? Or will we be forever captivated by the enormous shopping-mall boot and the retail booty that lies beyond? For some answers, let's look to a movie in theaters right now called "Confessions of a Shopaholic."

It is about Rebecca Bloomwood (Isla Fisher), a young professional who's addicted to shopping, considers $200 underwear a "basic human right" and offers pop wisdom like this: "A man will never love you or treat you as well as a store."

This is documentary masquerading as frothy screwball comedy. For Rebecca slowly begins to realize that her lust for purchasing is leading her to lie, ruin her finances and alienate the man she loves. Because she buys, her world comes crashing down. And it bewilders her. "When I shop," she says, "the world gets better. The world IS better. Then it's not anymore. And I need to do it again."

Funny thing, though, how the film's contradictions so starkly reflect our own at this moment in history. Rebecca's parents frequent thrift stores and flea markets, the out-of-touch but heartfelt vestiges of an America that once saved and reused. A debt collector who stalks Rebecca is an obnoxious nerd, because responsibility, after all, isn't cool. And at the end, when Rebecca makes her choice between shopping and love, her moral compass points right at the North Pole of traditional values.

Then the credits roll. And in the acknowledgments, the producers thank Prada and Fendi and Anna Sui.

"We have lived," Barack Obama said last month, "through an era where too often short-term gains were prized over long-term prosperity, where we failed to look beyond the next payment, the next quarter, or the next election." Is it any wonder that a society always so obsessed with the excitement of tomorrow somehow neglected the reality of it?

Something is at hand here. What it is—well, we are the ones charged with defining that. Where do we find our answers? In understanding better why we do what we do and buy what we buy? In the anger that hey—those government and corporate guys are spending beyond their means, and whoa, so are we?

Or is it all, in the time-honored American tradition, just a blip that we'll forget when the Dow rises and the banks resume lending and the leading economic indicators are once more pointing toward the sky?

Decision 2008 is behind us. Decision 2009 is of a different species. It is not either-or, not a horse race, not a sound bite. It is about how society—and that means he and she and, yes, you—is going to think about things like instant gratification and the hunger for newness and the envelopes with the glassine windows that keep arriving in the mail.

Carl George, the accountant, is what some of the TV financial talking heads like to call "cautiously optimistic" that we'll learn something here. "This is going to be permanently embedded in our minds—and should be," he says. "The key is to remember those lessons and pass those lessons on to the next generation."

In other words, thinking about the future, one of the most American things of all. It can save us or destroy us, depending on what we do next.

4

Americans Are Becoming More Frugal

Kimberly Palmer

Kimberly Palmer is a senior editor for U.S. News & World Report. *She commonly covers issues concerning the American economy.*

The economic recession of 2008 has forced many Americans to spend less and be more frugal with their incomes. Some people are trading in gas-guzzling cars, looking for free or low-cost entertainments, and eating out less often. Although this new thrift stems from the economic downturn, large numbers of Americans are also simply becoming disenchanted with consumer culture. They are learning that less clutter reduces their anxiety and that penny-pinching measures can even help the environment, giving themselves something to feel good about. However, the true test of this commitment to downsizing and financial responsibility will come when the recession ends and America may once again be faced with the temptations of easy credit and extra cash.

When it comes to longevity, few royals can top America's King Consumer. For more than four decades, our shopaholic nation has shown an insatiable desire to spend until our credit cards melt. And throughout this era, consumer spending has, well, *consumed* a greater and greater share of our total economy. Only twice since 1965, despite half a dozen recessions, have Americans spent less in a year than the previ-

Kimberly Palmer, "The End of Credit Card Consumerism," *U.S. News & World Report*, August 8, 2008. Copyright © 2008 U.S. News & World Report, L.P. Reprinted with permission.

ous one. Indeed, it often seems that we have defined ourselves by our ability to buy supersized everything, from McMansions to tricked-out SUVs to 60-inch flatscreen televisions—all enabled by decades of cheap credit.

On the surface, it may seem that there's nothing wrong with all that conspicuous consumption, especially for the biggest, most productive economy on the planet. After all, our undying love of stuff has helped fuel a global economic boom. Yet today, America finds itself at a once-or-twice-a-century economic tipping point. A sharp slowdown, record-high gas prices, high consumer debt levels, a plunging real estate market, and the growing green movement all seem to be conspiring to dethrone King Consumer and transform the economy and the American way of life for years to come. "The process of bringing our wants and our needs into realignment," says Merrill Lynch economist David Rosenberg, "is going to involve years of savings and frugality." Or, to put it more simply, "there is an anti-bling thing going on," says Marian Salzman, chief marketing officer of [public relations firm] Porter Novelli.

Consumers Are Forced to Scale Back

Many consumers, of course, don't have much choice but to scale back. Total credit card debt has increased by over 50 percent since 2000. The average American with a credit file is responsible for $16,635 in debt, excluding mortgages, according to Experian, and the personal savings rate has hovered close to zero for the past several years. High gas and food prices are causing real incomes to fall. Even worse, rising inflation will probably cause the Federal Reserve to start jacking up interest rates once the credit crisis on Wall Street has passed, tightening credit even further. "We're shedding jobs, it's much harder to borrow, and what used to be capital gains are now capital losses," says Scott Hoyt, senior director of consumer economics at Moody's Economy.com. "There's no source of funding for spending." Because many of us won't be able to as easily use our homes as ATMs, Hoyt expects to see an upward trend in saving and slower growth in consumer spending, compared with the binge of the past decade.

It was our appetite for housing, after all, that served as the catalyst for the multidecade consumer boom. Consider this: Consumer spending has risen to just over 70 percent of the U.S. economy from a bit more than 60 percent in 1965. The pace really picked up in the 1970s, when the first baby boomers started buying and furnishing their own homes. But now, Rosenberg says, the median boomer is in his early 50s and looking to unload his fleet of leased SUVs.

Total credit card debt has increased by over 50 percent since 2000.

To some degree, then, demographics are destiny. Longer term, an aging population will need to spend less and save more for retirement. As that process plays out, consumer spending may become less important in the big economic picture. Moody's Economy.com forecasts that the combination of demographic and financial factors will cause just such a seismic economic shift. Reversing a four-decade ascent, consumer spending could actually start falling as a percentage of U.S. gross domestic product, slipping to 68 percent over the next seven years.

Yearning for a Simpler Life

And this new frugality might actually be OK with many of us. Consumers were "so glutted on everything that they had acquired and all the time that was robbed from them . . . that they almost saw this [downturn] as a great opportunity to stop," says Faith Popcorn, chief executive of her eponymous consultancy. In a recent survey, she found that 90 percent of respondents said they were considering options for "the simpler life," and 84 percent said they were inclined to buy "less stuff."

Another survey found that people rank being in control of their finances and living a green lifestyle higher as signs of success than having money or a luxury car, and view having a paid-off mortgage as more of a status symbol than having a beautiful home. "We have to convince ourselves that the lifestyle we can afford right now is a desirable one," says Holly Heline Jarrell, a global director at the communications firm Manning Selvage & Lee, which sponsored the survey.

Examples of the mind-set shift abound. Large-vehicle sales declined 5.5 percent during the first six months of 2008, while compact-car sales rose 33 percent, according to J. D. Power & Associates. Piaggio, the company that makes Vespas, reports that scooter sales in June [2008] were up 146 percent over a year earlier. Even daily lattes have been cut; in July, Starbucks announced that it was closing 600 stores in response to reduced consumer traffic. The NPD Group [a market research firm] has found that the number of meals made at home has been steadily rising since 2001. "We're coming back to the home," says Harry Balzer, vice president of the firm.

[One recent] survey found that people rank being in control of their finances and living a green lifestyle higher as signs of success than having money or a luxury car, and view having a paid-off mortgage as more of a status symbol than having a beautiful home.

For some people, the downscaling has more to do with a changing definition of cool than with budgeting. The summer blockbuster *WALL-E* depicts a future world where spending and waste have spiraled so out of control that the Earth becomes a giant landfill. Magazines play up how celebrity moms like Victoria Beckham, aka Posh Spice, and Heidi Klum shop at Target for their kids. A simplification industry has spawned an annual Buy Nothing Day, books and blogs about not purchasing anything for a year, and *Real Simple* magazine. One recent post on the Consumerist, an irreverent website dedicated to standing up to corporations, contemplated the Geo Metro's transformation from "weak to chic." Consumerist's senior editor, Meg Marco, who used to drive the unstylish but fuel-efficient vehicle herself, says, "When gas is over $4 per gallon, I don't think anyone is any less 'cool' simply because they're seen driving a compact car."

Young consumers in their 20s may be most affected by the shift to simplicity. In focus group research for her upcoming book on generation Y, consumer psychologist Kit Yarrow has found growing interest in secondhand stores. Young shoppers tell her that it's a "way to get new stuff without creating stuff," she says. And because consumers often learn their lifetime shopping habits during their developmental years, Mandy Putnam, vice president at TNS RetailForward, says that members of generation Y may be permanently shaped by today's lessons in austerity, much as their great-grandparents were by the Great Depression.

Going Green

There's also an environmental component, says personal finance guru David Bach. "I just sat at the kitchen table with my 5-year-old son talking about 'reduce, reuse, recycle'—I couldn't have told you that at 5," Bach says. He recently wrote *Go Green, Live Rich*, which focuses on how helping the Earth can coincide with smart financial choices, such as avoiding bottled water and starting a vegetable garden.

Russell Simon, a 26-year-old communications manager for Carbonfund.org, a non-profit, embodies that way of thinking. He furnished his Washington, D.C., apartment with used furniture found on Craigslist, uses a canvas bag to bring home groceries, and gave up his '99 Subaru Impreza Wagon. He fills his time with activities, like swing dance lessons, that don't involve buying things. While he's glad his anticonsumption ways have a positive effect on the environment, Simon's motivations are more self-serving. "It's about uncluttering my mind, uncluttering my space, and allowing me to focus on things that matter," he says.

Cindee Mazzanti, a self-employed 57-year-old living in upstate New York, started downsizing in 2001, when the end of the dot-com bubble made her realize the importance of living within one's means. She sold her home and used the equity to pay off her debts and purchase a smaller home without a mortgage. She also traded in her Ford Freestyle SUV for a more thrifty Ford Focus to lower her own fuel costs and help reduce America's demand for foreign oil. Her monthly living expenses shrank from $5,600 to $1,200. Without debt, she says, she feels free.

But what happens when budgets aren't so tight? Plenty of hardheaded economists say we'll go right back to our prodigal ways.

The Struggle to Overcome Old Habits

Retailers are doing what they can to woo these new, economy-minded consumers. In April, Starbucks began offering new rewards on its stored-value cards, including free refills on hot and iced brewed coffee and complimentary syrup and soy milk. "This was an opportunity . . . to show Starbucks can be a part of people's lives even when budgets are tight," Brad Stevens, vice president of Starbucks's customer relationship management, says.

But what happens when budgets aren't so tight? Plenty of hardheaded economists say we'll go right back to our prodigal ways. Alan Blinder, economics professor at Princeton University and former Federal Reserve vice chairman, thinks that optimism and the drive to spend are hard-wired parts of America's cultural DNA. Blinder expects that even baby boomers will continue the spending spree that has defined most of their lives, buying medical care and golf vacations instead of new cars and larger homes.

Economist David Malpass argues that Americans aren't nearly as bad off as the low personal savings rate suggests because that calculation ignores the buildup of net worth. (If you bought a share of XYZ Corp. in January at $100, for instance, and its value doubled by December, the savings rate measure would still value that investment at $100.) Malpass points out that the average household has $573,379 in assets, including the value of retirement plans and the cash value of life insurance, and only $117,951 in liabilities.

Even if Americans do curtail their spendthrift habits, the result would probably be a healthier and more balanced American economy. Next year, the federal budget deficit is projected to reach almost $500 billion for the first time. America couldn't afford such a fiscal shortfall if foreign investors, such as the Chinese, didn't buy our debt—U.S. treasury bonds. If as a nation we bought a bit less and saved a bit more, economists say, the result would be stronger long-term economic growth. And depending on the kindness of strangers to perpetually finance your lavish spending sure seems risky. If the foreign appetite for U.S. dollar assets abated, says T. Rowe Price chief economist Alan Levenson, the dollar would probably weaken further, reducing Americans' standard of living.

Besides, there is more to the economy than just the consumer. The economic boom of the 1990s was led by business investment, especially in technology, aiding a boost in productivity that continues today. While businesses are holding back on investment because of recession fears, they are likely to beef it up after that threat passes, says Robert Brusca, chief economist at Fact and Opinion Economics.

And Uncle Sam may have a role to play as well by investing taxpayers' dollars to upgrade our national infrastructure and advance alternative energy technologies. "We're at a critical moment," says Benjamin Barber, author of *Consumed*. "In two or three years, we might say, 'We had a moment where the banks were broke, credit cards didn't have much credit left, when Americans were beginning to rethink consumerism, when we really could have turned the page,'" Barber says. "Or we might be saying, 'We talked ourselves back into the old fixes,'" such as rebate checks and even telling Americans directly to go out and spend, as President [George W.] Bush did after 9/11.

If as a nation we bought a bit less and saved a bit more, economists say, the result would be stronger long-term economic growth.

With baby boomers' habits well ingrained, it may instead be generation X and generation Y who decide to embrace a simpler, less wasteful lifestyle, rebelling against the conspicuous consumption that their parents helped make the American way of life.

5

The U.S. Should Reduce Oil Consumption in Favor of Cleaner Energy

Ron Wyden

Since 1996, Ron Wyden has served as a U.S. Senator for the State of Oregon. Wyden has been a consumer advocate and a promoter of health care reform during his tenure in Congress. As a founding member of the Oregon Gray Panthers, Wyden has also supported legislation securing the needs and rights of America's elderly.

America is addicted to oil, and the cost of that addiction lines the pockets of foreign oil producers at the expense of investing in homegrown alternative fuel technologies. The United States needs to develop alternative fuels for vehicles and build transit corridors that cater to automobiles and public transportation powered by these fuels. In addition, the country has to think more broadly about replacing fossil fuel technologies with wind, solar, biomass, and other relatively clean power resources. The government must support the marketing of alternative fuels and fund research into clean technologies to inspire U.S. industry to tackle current energy problems head-on. Only by mobilizing Americans behind the transition to alternative energies can the nation escape its reliance on expensive and ever-dwindling fossil fuels.

Americans consume too much oil, and they pay too high a price for it. National security pays a price. The environ-

Ron Wyden, "The Wyden Plan for Energy Independence," in senate.gov, May 20, 2009.

ment pays a price and the economy clearly pays a price. It's clear that Americans can no longer afford the energy policy of the status quo.

Last summer [in 2008], when crude oil prices approached $150 dollars a barrel, Americans were sending roughly $1.7 billion dollars a day to foreign countries to pay to cover their addiction to oil. That's $1.7 billion a day that was not invested here at home. Rather it went into the pockets of oil producers in foreign countries—and often to countries that oppose America's interests and undermine American security. A third of the oil Americans use comes from the OPEC [Organization of Petroleum Exporting Countries] oil cartel—a cartel that includes governments who are either openly hostile to the United States or who provide a haven and support to those who are. American dependence on their oil is a recipe for disaster.

The Costs of Oil Consumption

Oil prices have retreated, but America's addiction to oil has not let up. The nation's transportation system is almost entirely fueled by it. When the price of oil goes up, transportation costs go up, which means shipping costs and the cost of everything that has to be shipped goes up right along with it.

On top of all the other faults oil brings with it, burning fossil fuels is bad for our health and the health of our planet. Burning fossil fuels produces 86% of the man-made greenhouse gases released into the environment every year in the United States. Motor fuels have become cleaner over the years, but they still heat up the environment with greenhouse gases, just like burning coal at electric generation plants. Continuing to rely on energy sources that do harm to the air, land and water is a failed policy and bad for America's future.

Spelling out the problem, however, is the easy part. There is no silver bullet when it comes to remaking the way the entire nation consumes energy and encouraging the development of viable alternatives. No one person, organization or piece of legislation can do it alone.

If America is going to get on the path to real energy independence, Americans not only have to build that path, every American is going to have to commit to changing course in the way they use energy. And while I believe that government cannot simply legislate such transformative change, it is my view that government can provide the incentives and framework needed to empower Americans to rise to the challenge.

Continuing to rely on energy sources that do harm to the air, land and water is a failed policy and bad for America's future.

While I cannot tell you where the next advancement in green energy will come from, I know that given the right tools and incentives there is no limit to what American ingenuity can achieve. This is why today [May 20, 2009] I am offering a series of proposals to speed up our progress toward a cleaner energy future. My proposals address the spectrum of solutions needed to get there. They start with harnessing the intellectual power of our colleges and universities to invent new energy technologies. They create new incentives for businesses to turn those technologies into new energy products. And they give consumers incentives to buy and install those new energy technologies in their homes and businesses.

Towards a Renewable Fuel Standard

If America is going to cut back in its use of oil, then it needs to take a hard look at the single largest user of oil, the transportation sector. Today, I am proposing a three-pronged program to dramatically reduce the amount of oil Americans use every day to get to work, do their errands, and transport American products to market.

First, I propose to dramatically revise the Renewable Fuel Standard that now requires gasoline and diesel fuel providers to blend larger and larger amounts of ethanol and other biofuels into motor fuel. I strongly support the continued development of biofuels, especially those that do not require the use of food grains like corn and oils used to make them. But as we have seen in recent years, you can't divert large amounts of food grains and oils without impacting the supply and price of those commodities. Last year, nearly a third of the U.S. corn crop was used for ethanol production, leading to more expensive food for families at a time when they can least afford it. That doesn't make sense to me.

If America is going to cut back in its use of oil, then it needs to take a hard look at the single largest user of oil, the transportation sector.

The current standard also doesn't do enough to genuinely reduce the amount of oil being consumed. In part this is because fuels like ethanol simply do not contain as much energy per gallon as the gasoline it is intended to replace. The existing standard is aimed at replacing less than 15 percent of U.S. gasoline and diesel fuel with renewable fuels. I think we can do better, which is why my proposal aims to replace a third of those fuels with new low-carbon fuels. Right now a third of the United States gasoline is imported from OPEC countries. Let's aim to get this country off OPEC oil once and for all!

I want to make it clear that I am not proposing these changes because I am opposed to using renewable fuels. I have already introduced legislation—S. 536—to allow biomass from Federal lands to be used in the production of biofuels. Under the existing Renewable Fuel Standard, biomass from Federal lands is prohibited from being used as a renewable fuel. This makes no sense from either an energy perspective or an environmental perspective. Allowing for the use of fuel derived from biomass from Federal lands will reduce the threat of catastrophic wild fires, help make those forests healthier, and open up a variety of economic opportunities for hard hit rural communities. It is also a step towards a sound national energy policy.

However, if the U.S. is going to have a Renewable Fuel Standard for motor fuels, then it really ought to be a standard open to all renewable fuels, not just a chosen few. This is why my legislation would allow a range of energy sources to qualify as motor "fuels" including electricity for plug-in cars, methane to fuel compressed natural gas vehicles, and hydrogen for fuel cells. Initially, these low-carbon fuels could come from conventional sources, such as electricity from the electric grid, but eventually they would need to come from renewable energy sources.

Singling out ethanol as the only additive approved for motor fuel only creates a market for ethanol, which in turn discourages research and investment in other promising fuels. Creating a technology neutral "low-carbon" standard to replace traditional fossil fuels with alternative lower-carbon domestic fuels opens the door for a whole host of advancements and innovations yet unknown.

Creating a technology neutral "low-carbon" standard to replace traditional fossil fuels with alternative lower-carbon domestic fuels opens the door for a whole host of advancements and innovations yet unknown.

Building an Alternative Fuel Infrastructure

In addition to supplying new, cleaner, renewable transportation fuels, I will also be introducing legislation to authorize the U.S. Department of Transportation to designate "Energy Smart Transportation Corridors" so that these fuels will be readily available for consumers. By working with trucking companies, fuel providers, and State and local officials, the Transportation Department would establish which alternative fuels would be available and where they could be purchased. They would standardize other features such as weight limit standards geared towards reducing fossil fuel use and the release of greenhouse gases. The corridors would also include designation of other methods of freight and passenger transportation, such as rail or mass transit—to help reduce transportation fuel use.

Beyond empowering Americans to make more energy efficient choices, my legislation would make sure that energy efficient choices are within the reach of more Americans. Because I believe that energy efficient vehicles should not just be a luxury item for affluent Americans, I will be reintroducing legislation to provide tax credits to Americans who purchase fuel efficient vehicles. Vehicles getting at least 10% more than national average fuel efficiency would get a $900 tax credit. The credit would increase up to $2,500 as vehicle fuel efficiency increased. The bill also provides a tax credit for heavy truck owners to install fuel saving equipment. And it would increase both the gas guzzler tax and the civil penalty for vehicle manufacturers who miss their legally-required Corporate Average Fuel Economy (CAFE) requirements. The technology-neutral tax credit is designed to get more fuel-efficient vehicles on the road by making fuel-efficient vehicles an affordable choice for more Americans.

Home and Business Alternatives

But reducing oil use by the transportation sector alone is not enough. Some forty percent of energy use in the U.S. is consumed in buildings. So I am introducing legislation to empower American families—as well as small and mid-sized businesses—to save energy and install clean energy equipment. The "Re-Energize America Loan Program" will create a $10 billion revolving loan program to allow home and property owners and small and mid-sized businesses, schools, hospitals and others to make clean energy investments. This zero-interest loan program would be administered at the state level, not by bureaucrats in Washington, D.C. so it will be tailored to regional needs. It would be financed through the transfer of federal energy royalties paid on the production of coal, gas and oil, and renewable energy from federal land. It would empower Americans and businesses to help themselves and help their country start laying the groundwork for an entirely different energy future.

States like Oregon have enormous potential for development of renewable energy—solar, wind, geothermal, biomass, wave and tidal. The challenge is to find new ways to harness these energies. Renewable energy is also not just about fuel that goes into cars or electricity for homes or buildings. Renewable energy can also be used to heat homes and buildings, and power factories and businesses. So I am introducing legislation to provide tax credits for the production of energy from renewable sources, such as steam from geothermal wells, or biogas from feedlots or dairy farms that is sold directly to commercial and industrial customers. A separate credit would be available if this renewable energy is used right on site to heat a building or provide energy for the dairy.

The goal of this bill is to foster the development of new renewable energy technologies while expanding the market for renewable energy beyond the wind farms and electric generation plants already in place. The amount of the tax credit will no longer be tied to the way energy is produced but rather the amount of energy produced. This will help new energy technologies get in the game, and reward solutions that create the most energy. I am also introducing legislation to end the current tax penalty on biomass, hydroelectric, wave and tidal energies and other forms of renewable energy that are only eligible for half of the available Federal production tax credit. America needs all of these resources if it is going to move into a new energy future. My goal is to create a level playing field and give all of these technologies the full tax benefit in order to stimulate investment and get more renewable energy projects built.

One big advantage of renewable energy is that some form of it can be found on every corner, and in every corner of the country.

Americans Can Find Energy Solutions

One big advantage of renewable energy is that some form of it can be found on every corner, and in every corner of the country. Whether it's a solar panel on a home or store—or geothermal power plant—there is renewable energy potential virtually everywhere. One set of technologies that can make renewable energy even more available are energy storage technologies. These are solutions that can store solar energy during the day for use at night, or store wind energy when the wind blows, to be used when it doesn't.

Simply put, not enough attention has been paid to the use of energy storage technologies, which can also address daily and seasonal peaks in energy demand such as all of those air conditioners that Americans will soon be putting to good use during the summer's hottest days. Federal funding for energy storage technologies has been virtually nonexistent. So I am introducing legislation to create an investment tax credit that will help pay for the installation of energy storage equipment both by energy companies who connect it to the electric transmission and distribution system and for on-site use in buildings, homes, and factories. Any number of different types of storage technology can qualify—batteries, flywheels, pumped water storage, to name a few. The credit would be based on the energy stored, not on the technology used.

The goal throughout the bills I'm introducing today is not to pick winners and losers. The goal is to encourage innovation and installation.

Last but not least, America not only needs new solutions to our energy problems. It needs a skilled workforce to make them a reality. So, I am also proposing an "Energy Grant" Higher Education program to provide $300 million a year to America's colleges and universities to work on regional energy problems. This program is modeled on the highly successful SeaGrant research and education program that has been run by the U.S. Department of Commerce for more than 30 years and the SunGrant program established to research biofuels. The EnergyGrant program would fund groups of colleges and universities to do research and develop education programs aimed at unique opportunities and challenges in each region of the country. Why rely solely on the Federal Government research programs to come up with solutions for regional energy issues when labs and research departments at colleges and universities around the country can contribute to the effort?

The Senate Energy Committee has already adopted legislation I have proposed to create a $100 million a year, community college-based training program for skilled technicians to build, install and maintain the new American energy infrastructure of wind turbines, geothermal energy plants, fuel calls, and other 21st Century technologies. Without these skilled workers, this future will not happen and without effective training programs there won't be skilled workers to fill the jobs. I am also introducing this proposal as a stand-alone bill to help ensure that job training gets the attention that it needs. What good will "green jobs" do for Americans if Americans don't have the skills that these jobs will demand?

My goal in formulating this agenda has been to mobilize Americans and American resources to achieve authentic energy independence and a new energy future. To really accomplish this goal, I believe we must employ every tool at our disposal. But in the end the success or failure of any effort to transform the way Americans use energy will ultimately rest with the American people. There is no question that this won't be easy, but I have faith that the energy challenges facing the nation today are no match for the collective ingenuity, talent and energy of the American people. Let's put those resources to work."

6

U.S. Oil Consumption Harms National Security and the Environment

Christopher Beddor et al.

Christopher Beddor et al. are senior staff and research fellows with the Center for American Progress, a progressive public policy institute that informs government leaders and the public at large about important issues, such as energy security, and offers specific courses of action to resolve them.

America's oil dependence is costing the nation hundreds of billions of dollars every year. While the financial loss is great, Americans must also recognize that much of this money is going to oil-producing countries that are unfriendly to the United States. In addition, U.S. national security has been tied to the whims of these foreign producers as both military and civilian sectors need a constant supply of oil to work efficiently. Spikes in oil prices or even the cessation of flow from an antagonistic nation could put America at risk. The United States needs to adopt alternative fuels to wean itself from foreign oil. This will increase the nation's self-sufficiency and help lessen the environmental impact of fossil fuel use, which is another cost the United States must bear if oil dependency does not slacken.

Financial Costs

The United States' oil habit is no longer affordable. It imported 66 percent of the oil it consumed in 2008, which ac-

Christopher Beddor et al., *Securing America's Future: Enhancing Our National Security by Reducing Oil Dependence and Environmental Damage*, Washington, DC: Center for American Progress, 2009. Copyright © 2009 Center for American Progress. This material was created by the Center for American Progress. www.americanprogress.org.

counted for 16 percent of all import spending that year. This widens the U.S. annual trade deficit, weakens the American economy, and means that our credit bill could interfere with our political interests.

We spent a total of $2.3 trillion on crude oil over the past decade, and $1.5 trillion in nominal dollars on imports (see Figure 4 [not shown]). This spending has only increased over time: The United States tripled its oil imports from 1985 to 2008, while domestic production fell by nearly 50 percent. And in 2008 alone the United States purchased $357 billion worth of foreign crude oil—equivalent to 2.3 percent of our nation's gross domestic product and the highest level ever recorded (see Figure 5 [not shown]).

Climate and Environmental Costs

Oil consumption has had a devastating and widespread effect on the environment, too. Its production, transport, and combustion lead to wilderness destruction, pollution, and global warming. Seismic wave testing for feasibility studies for oil production in the Outer Continental Shelf disorients marine wildlife and has led to mass beaching of whales, while construction of major infrastructure on land—such as roads, jet landing strips, repair shops, homes, and industrial complexes—has destroyed natural habitats and been linked with cancer in wildlife.

> *Burning fossil fuels such as coal and oil constitute the greatest source of greenhouse gas emissions that cause global warming.*

A related concern is oil spills, which have resulted in mass mortality and contamination of wildlife, fish, and other food species in the ocean. The most recent spill occurred in July 2009, when a cracked underwater pipeline 33 miles off the Louisiana shore spilled 63,000 barrels of oil into the surrounding Gulf of Mexico. Mammals, reptiles, amphibians, and birds that live in or near the ocean are poisoned by oil waste from these spills. It damages the delicate ecosystem of our oceans and disrupts the food chain on which fish and sea creatures depend, and on which their reproduction is based.

Burning fossil fuels such as coal and oil constitute the greatest source of greenhouse gas emissions that cause global warming. The EIA found that "energy-related carbon dioxide emissions, resulting from the combustion of petroleum, coal, and natural gas, represented 82 percent of total U.S. anthropogenic greenhouse gas emissions in 2006."

National Security Costs

The United States will remain vulnerable to volatile oil prices and supply shortages as long as it heavily depends on other nations for fuel and energy. Its need for steady supplies of oil means it must adjust its behavior and strategies in order to maintain relations with less-than-savory regimes including Venezuela, Nigeria, and Russia. These countries, as well as smaller nations such as Angola, will therefore hold an increasingly disproportional amount of bilateral and regional power, while the United States has diminished leverage and constrained policy options in strategic regions such as the Middle East and Central Asia.

This trend will be exacerbated as continued depletion of oil production and exports from friendly regimes forces the United States to import more from antagonistic countries in the future in order to offset the tapering supply.

High rates of American consumption drive up global demand for oil, which fuels lofty prices and helps to fund and to sustain undemocratic and corrupt regimes.

Former military officials are speaking out on this issue. The CNA Military Advisory Board, a group of distinguished retired military leaders, issued a report in May 2009 arguing that America's reliance on foreign oil poses a serious threat to U.S. national security. The report, entitled "Powering America's Defense: Energy and the Risks to National Security," concluded that "U.S. dependence on oil weakens international leverage, undermines foreign policy objectives, and entangles America with unstable or hostile regimes."

America's oil dependence has other indirect but no less serious impacts on U.S. interests. For example, high rates of American consumption drive up global demand for oil, which fuels lofty prices and helps to fund and to sustain undemocratic and corrupt regimes. Because of this anti-Western nations such as Iran—with whom the United States by law cannot trade or buy oil—benefit regardless of who the end buyer of the fuel is.

Last year, record oil prices driven by global demand and speculators flooded Iran's treasury with oil money, which helped keep Mahmoud Ahmadinejad afloat. Prior to Iran's presidential election *The Economist* noted, "The president's open-handed economic policies, based on a windfall of $250 billion in oil sales during his four-year term and intended to redistribute wealth, have won friends among the poor."

Reducing U.S. oil demand in the world market would be a big financial hit to Iran and other unfriendly petrostates. And it would have the added benefit of making more fuel from stable nations available to countries such as China, which currently purchases from Iran and Sudan because U.S. demand dominates oil trade with friendly sources.

The revenues and power from oil exports also undermine American interests in rule of law, good governance, development, and democracy promotion around the world. Funds from oil exports are rarely distributed among the people of oil-exporting countries. They often stay concentrated in the hands of a small group of ruling elites who exploit oil revenues to preserve their hold on power.

In some cases oil revenues skew political processes and hinder good governance. As a Council on Foreign Relations report noted, "States that are politically unstable and poorly governed often struggle with the task of responsibly managing the large revenues that come from their oil and gas exports. . . . Production in fragile democracies, such as Nigeria, can be undermined when politicians or local warlords focus on ways to seize oil and gas rents rather than on the longer-term task of governance."

The revenues and power from oil exports also undermine American interests in rule of law, good governance, development, and democracy promotion around the world.

In another example, Angola—the sixth largest exporter of oil to the United States—remains one of the poorest nations with the highest mortality rate in the world, and its corrupt ruling regime continues to reject International Monetary Fund assistance.

The significant contribution of oil combustion to global warming leads to serious national security concerns as well. As mentioned earlier, oil consumption results in far-spanning and acute environmental damage, including global warming. In 2007, the CNA Military Advisory Board published a study on the effect of climate change on American security interests. Their study found that "climate change poses a serious threat to America's national security. . . . [It] acts as a threat multiplier for instability in some of the most volatile regions of the world."

It will:

- Create destabilizing conditions, including reduced access to fresh water, impaired food production, health catastrophes, and loss of land, which will place additional strains on weak governments.

- Exacerbate marginal living standards in developing countries in Asia, Africa, and the Middle East, creating widespread instability and increasing the likelihood of conflict, mass migrations, and failed states.

- Make Defense Department operations more vulnerable because extreme environmental conditions will considerably increase operation and maintenance costs, compromise seal-level military bases, complicate ship and aircraft operations, and expose the national power grid upon which DoD is heavily reliant.

These findings were backed up by a 2007 Center for American Progress report, "The Security Challenges of Climate Change," which in addition to these findings identified other effects on national security. These included "increased U.S. border stress due to the severe effects of climate change in parts of Mexico and the Caribbean" and a "strain on the capacity of the United States—and in particular the U.S. military—to act as a 'first responder' to international disasters and humanitarian crises due to their increased frequency, complexity, and danger."

A few weeks ago retired Admiral Dennis McGinn re-emphasized these key points in testimony before the Senate Foreign Relations Committee. He stressed that climate change places our military in jeopardy and is enormously expensive; our reliance on fossil fuels compromises our foreign policy and international leverage; and fossil fuels make the U.S. economy vulnerable to sudden shocks.

Some critics argue that the United States should not deal with this issue now and instead rely on investments in clean-energy technology and voluntary measures to reduce pollution. But this approach failed over the last eight years. In fact, venture capitalist John Doerr of Kleiner, Perkins told the Senate that "We must put a price on carbon and a cap on carbon emissions," to spur investments in the clean-energy technologies of the future.

We should heed expert advice and take action now to significantly reduce oil use and reduce global warming pollution. Transitioning to a low-carbon economy and reducing America's dependence on foreign imports in the process isn't just vital for our environment—it's vital for our security.

7

U.S. Consumption of Oil Is Declining

Steve Everly

Steve Everly is a writer for the Kansas City Star *and his work is syndicated in other local papers. He often writes on energy issues.*

As the price of gasoline has risen steadily over the past decade, U.S. oil consumption has declined. Refineries are underproducing because consumers cannot or will not pay the high cost of gas. Many consumers are shedding gas-guzzling vehicles or cutting down on travel to save the expense; others are switching to automobiles run on alternative fuels. The government is responding to this change by investing in alternative fuels such as ethanol, making more stringent demands for fuel-efficient vehicles, and inducing car companies to increase their alternative-fuel fleets.

The United States used more gasoline than ever in 2007 and far more than any other country. It seemed as if America's growing appetite for gas would go on forever.

Well, it won't—and things may never be the same.

Gasoline consumption has been down the last two years, in part because of the recession. Even when the economy picks up, three underlying trends mean the United States might never use as much gas again:

- New standards for cars and light trucks, including SUVs, will make U.S. vehicles more fuel-efficient.

- The growth in the number of U.S. vehicles, after surging the last 30 years, is likely to plateau. The country now has more than four vehicles for every five people, including children.

- Alternative fuels will grow enough to cover increased fuel needs.

As a result, the federal Energy Information Administration predicts that 2007 was the peak year for U.S. gasoline demand. Even in 2035, the last year of the latest long-term projections, motorists are expected to use less gasoline than they are now.

As unexpected as this trend was, there is widespread agreement that it is right.

"We're on a slow but inexorable path away from petroleum. This is a big deal," said James Williams, an analyst with WTRG Economics, an oil and gas consultancy.

In a recent speech in Washington, D.C., Rex Tillerson agreed.

"Motor vehicle gasoline demand is down, is headed down and is going to continue to head down," said Tillerson, the CEO of Exxon Mobil Corp., the world's largest oil company.

Refineries now use only 78.5 percent of their capacity, the lowest level since the federal government began routinely collecting the information in 1990.

Refineries Are Operating Under Capacity

That decline is reverberating through the oil industry. Refineries now use only 78.5 percent of their capacity, the lowest level since the federal government began routinely collecting the information in 1990. Valero Energy, which once bought refineries enthusiastically, now snaps up ethanol plants instead.

And Chevron Corp. recently announced it was reorganizing its U.S. refining business, which could include selling or closing refineries.

One variable will be how quickly consumers take to alternatives and more-efficient vehicles.

When the new fuel-economy standards were being considered, a Gallup poll found 80 percent of respondents supported the idea, even though it could make vehicles smaller and more expensive. A Pew Research Center poll released last week [February 2010] found only 49 percent of respondents said they favored making energy a top priority, down from 60 percent a year ago.

Mike Omotoso, an analyst for the marketing firm J.D. Power & Associates, said many consumers are reluctant to pay more for alternatives such as electric hybrids, especially when gas costs less than $3 a gallon.

"People can have short memories," Omotoso said.

Everyone knows the era of $2 gas is over.

Other analysts say $4 gasoline left a lasting impression. Mike Right, a spokesman for AAA [Automobile Association of America], said consumers understand things have changed and higher energy prices weren't a temporary situation.

"Everyone knows the era of $2 gas is over," he said.

Signs of Change

Paul Gilbert, a former area resident who is now retired in southern Missouri, makes regular trips to Kansas City in his pickup truck—trips that became especially pricey when gas prices spiked in 2008. Though gas prices have settled, Gilbert said they're still too high, and he plans to buy a Honda Accord or Toyota Corolla.

"You either do what is right or keep on going down the path we're going down," he said. "People are starting to wise up."

Americans have tried this before. In the 1970s after the OPEC [Organization of Petroleum Exporting Countries] oil embargo, the government imposed fuel-efficiency standards and other measures to slash fuel and oil consumption. The effort eventually was undone by plummeting oil prices and the popularity of thirsty SUVs.

Federal tax incentives for ethanol, though widely criticized, have helped increase production from less than 1 billion gallons in 1992 to 10.5 billion [in 2009].

The experience left a lesson that is playing out again. Forward-looking policies require patience and can be difficult politically, but they pay off, said Jay Hakes, a former head of the Energy Information Administration and the author of *A Declaration of Energy Independence*.

"It's a gradual thing," Hakes said. "The really good policies are the ones that look five to 10 years ahead."

A similar approach is showing results. Federal tax incentives for ethanol, though widely criticized, have helped increase production from less than 1 billion gallons in 1992 to 10.5 billion last year [in 2009]. That reduces by 5 percent the amount of gas the country needs.

The new fuel-efficiency standards won't be fully felt for years.

Congress approved the measure in 2007, and the [Barack] Obama administration toughened it by saying the standard must be fully in force by 2016 instead of 2020. Fuel efficiency must start climbing in the 2011 model year, and by 2016, cars are to average 39 miles per gallon and light trucks, including SUVs, must average 30 miles per gallon. The current requirements are 27.5 mpg for cars and 23.1 for light trucks.

How much fuel will that save? The 2011 models, according to federal estimates, will save 900 million gallons over their lifetimes. That's not bad, but it amounts to only a day's worth of U.S. oil consumption.

By 2016, the results are more impressive. All the vehicles produced under the new standards are expected to save 76 billion gallons of gas. That impact will build for a few more years, because it takes about 20 years to completely replace the nation's vehicles.

Meanwhile, a decline in the number of vehicles owned by U.S. households will have an impact. From 1980 to 2007, 100 million vehicles were registered in the U.S., giving the country 844 vehicles for every 1,000 people. As a result, car travel nearly doubled to 3 trillion miles a year.

Last year, the number of vehicles in the U.S. dipped slightly, J.D. Power said, and just slowing the growth in vehicles should help prevent a surge in gasoline demand.

All of that doesn't mean gasoline will stay cheap, because growing demand in countries such as China and India eventually will send prices back up.

And it doesn't mean gas will disappear. The Energy Information Administration predicts that by 2035, petroleum still will provide 88 percent of the fuel for cars and light trucks.

The Growth of Alternative Fuels

The rest will come from alternative fuels—mainly ethanol, followed by electricity, natural gas, hydrogen and propane. Many analysts say alternatives will grow much faster than federal officials expect. That will depend in part on developing infrastructure such as stations to charge electric cars or dispense compressed natural gas.

Several alternate fuels could enjoy some growth, said Mary Beth Stanek, the director of environment, energy and safety policy for General Motors Corp. GM expects hydrogen to play a bigger role and has a second generation of hydrogen cars in the field.

However quickly alternatives are adopted, they mean less gasoline use—and a reshuffling of past expectations.

In 2005, the chief executive of the largest independent U.S. refining company, Valero, declared a "Golden Age of refining" and said the best was yet to come. Less than five years later, Valero has a new CEO—who says that age is over.

When Valero spokesman Bill Day was asked last week whether his company agreed that demand for gas will drop, he put it this way:

"It makes sense to us."

8

Americans Eat Too Much

Adrienne Forman

Adrienne Forman is a consultant and freelance writer, specializing in health communications. She is the editor of the Shape Up America! *newsletter, and has been a contributing editor of the* Environmental Nutrition *newsletter for the past 14 years. She is a former senior nutritionist at Weight Watchers International.*

Americans are experiencing an obesity epidemic because of overeating and lack of physical exercise. Foods rich in calories are available everywhere and at low cost, so it is easy to overeat. Modern technology and lifestyle encourage a lack of physical activity. The solution is to eat less and be more active. Americans could put an end to the average yearly weight gain by following the advice of James O. Hill, director of the Center for Human Nutrition at the University of Colorado Health Sciences Center, who established the America on the Move program. The essence of this program is to burn 100 calories more per day through physical activity and to eat 100 fewer calories per day.

Americans are fat and getting fatter. Is that the result of bad genes or the American way? We all know the answer. It's not hard to see that our current way of life encourages overeating and discourages physical activity. The result is inevitable—an obesity epidemic fueled by our lifestyle not our DNA. The bestseller *French Women Don't Get Fat* (Knopf, 2005) trades on this premise.

What can we do about it? Fight back! Sure, the temptations to eat as well as to remain sedentary are all around, whether you're at home, on the job or in transit. There's easy access to tasty, calorie-dense foods at supermarkets, gas stations and even bookstore cafes. And it takes willpower not to be seduced with inexpensive, supersized portions by counter salespeople who coo, "It's only 10 cents more."

Get a Move On. Inactivity is now as much an American trademark as fast food. To save precious time, we drive instead of walk, take elevators instead of stairs and use technology like e-mail that eliminates even the walk to the mailbox. When we manage to catch a break from our hectic day, we relax by watching TV or surfing the Internet. Even when you want to go for a walk, a lack of sidewalks in some locations, poor street lighting or unsafe neighborhoods are obstacles. It's no wonder there's a public health crisis. Americans need to band together and emulate Peter Finch in the movie "Network" by opening the window and shouting "I'm mad as h——, and I'm not going to take it any more!"

The 100-Calorie Solution. To counter the cultural forces that encourage Americans to put on pounds, James O. Hill, Ph.D., director of the Center for Human Nutrition at the University of Colorado Health Sciences Center in Denver, says we need to find a better balance between how much we eat and move.

The temptations to eat as well as to remain sedentary are all around, whether you're at home, on the job or in transit.

Using data from two national surveys, he estimates that eliminating just 100 calories a day—by moving more and eating less—could prevent weight gain in most people. In other words, small changes in behavior could close the 100-calorie-a-day gap and stop the average weight gain of one to three pounds a year.

Hill's America on the Move (AOM) program, a national initiative, has a simple message: To prevent weight gain, walk 2,000 more steps and eat 100 fewer calories each day. (Because this cuts 100 calories and burns 100 calories, you'll be successful even if you fall a bit short on either one.) How to do it? Walk an extra mile (about 15 to 20 minutes of brisk walking) and eliminate the equivalent of three teaspoons of butter or margarine daily.

The idea is catching on. Currently, 17 states and two cities are taking on the AOM challenge to build community programs that support healthy eating and active living. For more information, visit the website www.americaonthemove.org.

Small Changes, Big Rewards

It doesn't take much to walk 2,000 more steps or eat 100 fewer calories a day. Small changes add up quickly. Try fitting these tips into your daily routine.

Add more steps:

- Wear a step-counter. (Need one? Visit www.america-onthemove.org or try a sporting goods store.)

- Listen to music while walking, but be sure to stay aware of cars and bicycles.

- Raining or too cold? Walk the mall. Or hit the treadmill at the gym.

- Get off the bus one stop before your destination and walk the rest of the way.

- Find friends or co-workers who want to walk as well. Meet at a set time and place; it makes it harder to cancel.

- Vacuum, mow the lawn, rake leaves, make a few trips carrying laundry up the stairs—household activities add steps too.

Eat fewer calories:

- Fill an omelet with mixed vegetables, spinach or mushrooms instead of cheese.

- When cooking, replace butter with nonstick cooking spray. At the table, use diet margarine or no-calorie butter spray.

- Choose nonfat milk instead of 2% milk, unsweetened yogurt with fresh fruit instead of sweetened fruit-flavored yogurt, part-skim instead of full-fat cheese.

- Make sandwiches with mustard or light mayonnaise instead of regular mayo.

- Limit meat portions to the size of your palm, limit potatoes and rice to half the size of a baseball.

- When eating out, eat only until you're comfortably full. Take the rest home for a "free" lunch the next day. Share an entree or dessert.

- At fast-food restaurants, order the smallest entree, side dish and beverage.

9

Americans Waste Too Much Food

Andrew Martin

Andrew Martin covers the food and beverage industries for The New York Times. *Before joining* The Times *in 2007, Martin worked at* The Chicago Tribune *for fourteen years, covering food policy and agriculture in the Washington bureau and politics at Chicago's City Hall.*

More than a quarter of the food prepared for consumption in America ends up in landfills. This waste of food is distressing because much of it could be recovered to feed hungry Americans. Many Americans, concerned by news of the obesity statistics, are more inclined to throw away leftovers than to eat them the next day. And restaurants and supermarkets tend to throw away unsold food rather than sell it and risk customers getting sick. A few programs are now recycling food waste and turning it into livestock feed and compost, but these efforts should be magnified. In addition, Americans need to take to heart the lesson of eating less and wasting less.

Grocery bills are rising through the roof. Food banks are running short of donations. And food shortages are causing sporadic riots in poor countries through the world.

You'd never know it if you saw what was ending up in your landfill. As it turns out, Americans waste an astounding amount of food—an estimated 27 percent of the food available for consumption, according to a government study—and it happens at the supermarket, in restaurants and cafeterias and in your very own kitchen. It works out to about a pound of food every day for every American.

Grocery stores discard products because of spoilage or minor cosmetic blemishes. Restaurants throw away what they don't use. And consumers toss out everything from bananas that have turned brown to last week's Chinese leftovers. In 1997, in one of the few studies of food waste, the Department of Agriculture estimated that two years before, 96.4 billion pounds of the 356 billion pounds of edible food in the United States was never eaten. Fresh produce, milk, grain products and sweeteners made up two-thirds of the waste. An update is under way.

The study didn't account for the explosion of ready-to-eat foods now available at supermarkets, from rotisserie chickens to sandwiches and soups. What do you think happens to that potato salad and meatloaf at the end of the day?

Edible Food Ends Up in Landfills

A more recent study by the Environmental Protection Agency estimated that Americans generate roughly 30 million tons of food waste each year, which is about 12 percent of the total waste stream. All but about 2 percent of that food waste ends up in landfills; by comparison, 62 percent of yard waste is composted.

The numbers seem all the more staggering now, given the cost of groceries and the emerging food crisis abroad.

A . . . recent study by the Environmental Protection Agency estimated that Americans generate roughly 30 million tons of food waste each year.

After President [George W.] Bush said recently that India's burgeoning middle class was helping to push up food prices by demanding better food, officials in India complained that not only do Americans eat too much—if they slimmed down to the weight of middle-class Indians, said one, "many people in sub-Saharan Africa would find food on their plate"—but they also throw out too much food.

And consider this: the rotting food that ends up in landfills produces methane, a major source of greenhouse gases.

America's Second Harvest—The Nation's Food Bank Network, a group of more than 200 food banks, reports that donations of food are down 9 percent, but the number of people showing up for food has increased 20 percent. The group distributes more than two billion pounds of donated and recovered food and consumer products each year.

The rotting food that ends up in landfills produces methane, a major source of greenhouse gases.

The problem isn't unique to the United States.

In England, a recent study revealed that Britons toss away a third of the food they purchase, including more than four million whole apples, 1.2 million sausages and 2.8 million tomatoes. In Sweden, families with small children threw out about a quarter of the food they bought, a recent study there found.

Recovering Wasted Food

And most distressing, perhaps, is that in some parts of Africa a quarter or more of the crops go bad before they can be eaten. A study presented last week to the United Nations Commission on Sustainable Development found that the high losses in developing nations "are mainly due to a lack of technology and infrastructure" as well as insect infestations, microbial growth, damage and high temperatures and humidity.

For decades, wasting food has fallen into the category of things that everyone knows is a bad idea but that few do anything about, sort of like speeding and reapplying sunscreen. Didn't your mother tell you to eat all the food on your plate?

Food has long been relatively cheap, and portions were increasingly huge. With so much news about how fat everyone was getting—66 percent of adult Americans are overweight or obese, according to 2003–04 government health survey—there was a compelling argument to be made that it was better to toss the leftover deep-dish pizza than eat it again the next day.

For decades, wasting food has fallen into the category of things that everyone knows is a bad idea but that few do anything about.

For cafeterias, restaurants and supermarkets, it was just as easy to toss food that wasn't sold into trash bins than to worry about somebody getting sick from it. And then filing a lawsuit.

"The path of least resistance is just to chuck it," said Jonathan Bloom, who started a blog last year called wastedfood.com that tracks the issue.

Of course, eliminating food waste won't solve the problems of world hunger and greenhouse-gas pollution. But it could make a dent in this country and wouldn't require a huge amount of effort or money. The Department of Agriculture estimated that recovering just 5 percent of the food that is wasted could feed four million people a day; recovering 25 percent would feed 20 million people.

The Department of Agriculture said it was updating its figures on food waste and officials there weren't yet able to say if the problem has gotten better or worse.

In many major cities, including New York, food rescue organizations do nearly all the work for cafeterias and restaurants that are willing to participate. The food generally needs to be covered and in some cases placed in a freezer. Food rescue groups pick it up. One of them, City Harvest, collects excess food each day from about 170 establishments in New York.

> *The Department of Agriculture estimated that recovering just 5 percent of the food that is wasted could feed four million people a day.*

"We're not talking about table scraps," said Joel Berg, executive director of the New York City Coalition Against Hunger, explaining the types of wasted food that is edible. "We're talking about a pan of lasagna that was never served."

Proper Food Recycling

For food that isn't edible, a growing number of states and cities are offering programs to donate it to livestock farmers or to compost it. In Massachusetts, for instance, the state worked with the grocery industry to create a program to set aside for composting food that can't be used by food banks.

"The great part about this is grocers save money on their garbage bill and they contribute a product to composting," said Kate M. Krebs, executive director of the National Recycling Coalition, who calls the wasting of food "the most wrenching issue of our day."

The City of San Francisco is turning food waste from residents and restaurants into tons of compost a day. The city has structured its garbage collection system so that it provides incentives for recycling and composting.

There are also efforts to cut down on the amount of food that people pile on their plates. A handful of restaurant chains including T.G.I. Friday's are offering smaller portions. And a growing number of college cafeterias have eliminated trays, meaning students have to carry their food to a table rather than loading up a tray.

"It's sort of one of the ideas you read about and think, 'Why didn't I think of that?'" Mr. Bloom said.

Countering the Waste Mentality

The federal government tried once before, during the [Bill] Clinton administration, to get the nation fired up about food waste, but the effort was discontinued by the Bush administration. The secretary of agriculture at the time, Dan Glickman, created a program to encourage food recovery and gleaning, which means collecting leftover crops from farm fields.

He assigned a member of his staff, Mr. Berg, to oversee the program, and Mr. Berg spent the next several years encouraging farmers, schools, hospitals and companies to donate extra crops and food to feeding charities. A Good Samaritan law was passed by Congress that protected food donors from liability for donating food and groceries, spurring more donations.

"We made a dent," said Mr. Berg, now at the New York City hunger group. "We reduced waste and increased the amount of people being fed. It wasn't a panacea, but it helped."

With the current food crisis, it seems possible that the issue of food waste might have more traction this time around.

Mr. Bloom said he was encouraged by the increasing Web chatter about saving money on food, something that used to be confined to the "frugal mommy blogs."

"The fundamental thing that I'm fighting against is, 'why should I care? I paid for it,'" Mr. Bloom said. "The rising prices are really an answer to that."

10

Americans Are Hoarding and Storing More Stuff Than Ever Before

Martin John Brown

Martin John Brown is a writer and researcher who focuses on historical and environmental subjects. His work has appeared in Air & Space, E/The Environmental Magazine, Smithsonian, *and other magazines.*

The self-storage boom in the United States testifies to Americans' love of hoarding and storing things. Though most people do not like clutter, they are uneasy with the notion of parting with belongings that they have accumulated over the years. Some dream that they will find a use for the items when they get bigger homes; others attach sentiment to objects that remind them of loved ones or happy times. Whatever the reason, Americans are content to pay rent to store items that they may not see or use for years.

A strange new shadow land has grown up in America. It's a world of cinderblock villas and plywood hallways, garish under halogen security bulbs. It clings to the underside of Western towns like Roman catacombs, pushes up funereal fault blocks in urban centers, and festoons suburban freeways with palaces styled after castles and forts. If you could peer inside those locked rooms, you'd see, well, practically any object you could imagine: a pair of skis, five toadstool-style cookie

Martin John Brown, "Too Much Stuff! America's New Love Affair with Self-Storage," AlterNet, June 4, 2008. Reproduced by permission of the author.

jars, twelve years' back issues of *Martha Stewart Living*, a single broken bed frame, all waiting like Egyptian tomb dressing to serve in some afterlife. But you'd rarely see a person, because all these new, gray places are for stuff.

The "self storage" business started small three or four decades ago, as a few "mini-warehouses" around military bases in the Southwest, according to industry legend. Now it's a $22 billion-per-year industry, and maybe a whole way of life. Like VCRs and cell phones, self-storage is a product Americans didn't need until they discovered it, and now they can't live without.

Building to Meet the Demand

The numbers are astounding. According to the Self Storage Association, an industry advocacy group, square footage of rentable storage has increased 740 percent in the past two decades; a *billion* square feet of storage space was created between 1998 and 2005; and there are now 6.8 square feet of storage for every man, woman and child in America. Chris Sonne, a storage expert at Cushman & Wakefield Inc., estimates there are 45,000 storage facilities today compared to zero 50 years ago.

"That's a pace of two or more self-storage facilities opening every day for 50 years," he says. "That beats McDonald's."

It's been a great ride for savvy investors, who watched the business produce impressive rents from inexpensive buildings. Industry giant Public Storage Inc. had total returns of 41 percent, 33 percent, 25 percent and 47 percent for the years 2003—2006, according to Morningstar. Though growth has slowed recently, due to high supply and tight credit, it hasn't stopped, with new development continuing in little-served areas like urban centers. What the hell is going on? Why do Americans crave all this space when they apparently lived fine without it 30 years ago?

There aren't many answers in the press. Storage tends to make the news only when something criminal or titillating happens—like when a murderer stores body parts in his unit, or Paris Hilton forgets to pay her rent, and her purported party photos and Amsterdam drug notes are auctioned off to the highest bidder.

Why do Americans crave all this space when they apparently lived fine without it 30 years ago?

I walk into the office of a Public Storage facility and talk to "Jack," the manager on duty. (He tells me he could get fired if I used his real name.) With his beard neatly trimmed and his shirt tucked in, he seems grounded and efficient. I ask why demand for his service is so big.

"I guess there are just a lot of pack rats out there," he says without skipping a beat.

That's the same initial reaction I got from the majority of the 20 people I talked to for this story, from Wall Street analysts to everyday customers. But draw those conversations out a bit, and those pack rats "out there" start looking like everyone you know. The problem isn't just with the crass and slavish mob; more thoughtful types use self-storage too.

Life Events That Create Unexpected Clutter

Part of the storage boom comes from use by business: Self Storage Association President Michael Scanlon says that perhaps 30 percent of customers are businesses storing records, equipment, inventory and the like. Still, the lion's share of the expansion has come from plain old folks storing their possessions. And every one of them has a story when they show up at Jack's desk.

"When people come in here, they are stressed out," he says. "Maybe their grandma died and left some furniture. Maybe they're moving. Maybe they got a new job."

These are "life events" in the parlance of industry analysts, and they're a gateway into the self-storage universe. Whether the event is good or bad, its high emotions come loaded with the job of dealing with a small mountain of stuff. That's where Jack can step in. A big part of a storage manager's job is unlicensed crisis counseling—talking the client down a bit, figuring out their plans for the next few hours or months, and getting their possessions off their hands so they can move on with their lives.

Getting into self-storage is so easy it can be a big relief to someone in the throes of a "life event." . . . It's getting out that can be the challenge.

"When they leave the office," Jack says, "I want to make sure at least this one thing is resolved for them." Like all of the self-storage managers I met, he is a down-to-earth, no-nonsense person who seems truly interested in helping.

Getting into self-storage is so easy it can be a big relief to someone in the throes of a "life event." There is no need to bother friends or family. There are few, if any, credit checks, reference checks, deposits or long-term leases. The service looks cheap, with typical monthly rents from 50 cents to 2 dollars per square foot. It's getting out that can be the challenge.

Consider a customer like Raeven (yes, her real name), now a preschool worker in Portland, Ore. Nine months ago she was in Ann Arbor, Mich., having a "life event." Her marriage was going to pieces. She retreated to her parents' home in Salem, Ore., and got her stuff into storage there. After a few months, she moved to Portland to start a new life. Now she occasionally goes down to Salem to retrieve things. On a recent visit she extracted some kitchen gear, some books on Jewish studies and 50 pairs of shoes. (There are more.) Her idea is to extricate the rest of the stuff and be out of the unit in a few months. It's a typical plan—and if Raeven is a typical client, she won't succeed.

"You start off by asking, 'how long do you plan on renting it for?'" says Scanlon. "Almost everybody says 'a month or two.'"

They end up staying a lot longer. Average tenancies nationwide are somewhere between one and two years, say Scanlon and Sonne, and some renters simply never leave.

"I have one renter who's been here since we opened—in 1990," says Dawn Spencer, a manager at Clackamas River Mini Storage outside of Portland. "He pays automatically, by credit card, never comes in. Lives in another state now."

"It's an industry that builds on inertia," says Paul Adornato, an analyst for BMO Capital Markets. "People would much rather have $150 withdrawn automatically out of their checking account every month than have to wake up on a Saturday morning, rent a truck, move out the stuff, do something with the stuff . . . see what I mean?"

Too Much Stuff in American Homes

One factor that does *not* explain the storage boom is lack of space in American houses. Over the last three decades, the average new American home has grown by about 900 square feet, according to [U.S.] Census data, while the number of people per household has declined slightly.

"Most of the people we rent to have a garage, an attic and a basement—can you believe that?" says Scanlon. Seventy-five percent of them own their own homes, he says. They simply have more and more stuff to wrangle. Rick, a real estate agent in Macomb County, Mich., is one such "premium residential customer," as Scanlon calls them. He's familiar with self-storage from his job, where he encourages customers to use storage to remove nonessential items and "stage" their homes for sale. He even plays a "decluttering" game with customers a few months later, after the sale, when they're ready to reclaim that excess. Can they even remember what's in there? Almost never, he says.

Rick had his own storage-inducing life event when he moved his father-in-law, who has "a touch of Alzheimer's," into assisted living.

One factor that does not *explain the storage boom is lack of space in American houses.*

"His house was a nightmare when we moved him out," relates Rick. "His basement was full of crap. His garage was full of crap. His extra bedrooms were full of crap. It's like, 'What do you need this stuff for?'" There wasn't room for it all in his assisted-living apartment, but Rick says his father-in-law couldn't distinguish between irreplaceable items, like old pictures, and replaceable junk like a prefab shelving unit. He wanted to keep it all.

Still, Rick and his wife couldn't exactly throw that crap away. On occasion, the father-in-law asked for specific things—an old picture, or a book—and they could hardly deny him such wishes. Rick didn't want to clutter up his own house. A storage unit was the logical solution. Getting a second unit seemed logical, too, when Rick's college-age son went abroad to study and left some things behind—furniture for his future apartment.

Finally, there was an incident in Rick's garage, which was getting a little crowded with his own stuff. A pile of it fell over and nearly damaged his prized MG roadster. Rick broke the mental seal and put some of his own stuff—some sports gear and old business papers—in his father-in-law's unit.

"I've encroached on it 30 percent," he says. Then he works out some math about his storage expenses.

"There's a bit of me that says—gosh, I'm paying, combined, about $100 a month. . . . I've been doing this for three years. . . ."

He trails off before he gets to the surprisingly large total.

I ask if the stuff in his two units is worth anything near $3,600.

"Nope."

Will he keep a storage unit when his father-in-law passes on and his son gets an apartment?

"Probably," he says, after some fumbling. "Just a smaller one."

The Hoarding Instinct

I can't help but get the impression that, like Rick, a good many Americans are in danger of literally getting pushed out of their houses by stuff. It seems odd in a time when eBay, craigslist, freecycle.org and charity pickup services make getting rid of possessions easier than ever.

Adornato has been thinking about those services too.

"All of that helps us to rotate our personal inventories," he says, "but ultimately, we like to accumulate."

The deluge of stuff springs from a combination of instinct and economics, says Cindy Glovinsky, a psychotherapist and author of *Making Peace With the Things in Your Life*. Humans are programmed to hoard, she says, and "things have gotten cheaper, and more widely available, and more quickly available than ever in history."

It hasn't helped, she thinks, that so many households now have two wage earners. Homemakers used to have time to sort through things and edit them. "But when you work all day," she says, "it seems like a huge burden." Especially when those two wage earners might have completely different ideas about their possessions.

For Eden, a hi-tech sales rep in Boston, her life event came two years ago when she moved from Idaho to Boston so her husband could go to grad school. It meant downsizing from a big suburban house to a standard apartment. There was no way all her husband's things, including a full cocktail bar setup—he is a mixing aficionado—could come with them.

"My impulse was to get rid of all that stuff and simplify," she says, "but he just has this gene that makes him accumulate stuff."

The compromise was leaving the bar, some furniture, tools and other miscellany in storage in Idaho, a place they weren't likely to live again, ever. It's still there today, rent prepaid, waiting to be rediscovered and reanimated. On some days, thinking about it bothers Eden a lot.

"People in third world countries couldn't even fathom this," she says. "Their houses aren't even as big as our storage unit."

Nonetheless, the storage unit has its usefulness. It prevents a major relationship crisis. And it makes a little down payment on a dream she and her husband have of building a beach house in British Columbia. When they get around to doing that, Eden says, all that stuff could be really useful.

The first step in addressing a problem with stuff . . . is not hiring a dump truck, but acknowledging the powerful emotional interactions everyone has with things.

Forming a Bond with Stuff

What's in storage, says Scanlon, doesn't often have great cash value. "It's mostly stuff people have an emotional attachment to," he says. "They think, 'I might need this someday, or the kids might want this.'. . . That's really what is motivating this."

It doesn't matter if such ideas are patently unrealistic, says Glovinsky: "Parents ought to ask, how much is the kid really going to want?" Rather, she says, they're powerful impulses, tied to instincts about survival and relationships.

"It's normal for people to be attached to objects," she says. "We tend to make do with them as people substitutes, like children with teddy bears, or [actor] Tom Hanks with his volleyball (in *Cast Away*). We all do some of that; it's really just a matter of degree."

The first step in addressing a problem with stuff, she emphasizes, is not hiring a dump truck, but acknowledging the powerful emotional interactions everyone has with things. Once you do that, it's easier to be selective—to pick some objects that represent memories or people or plans for the future, and get rid of the rest.

A Global Phenomenon

It seems so easy to blame the ugly, consuming American for the storage boom, to see spending $50 or $150 a month to store junk as a spiritual failing unique to the United States. But Americans aren't storing junk, they're storing dreams—of days when there will be a better house to move in to, of days with time to read all those magazines and make all those recipes; of kids who honor family ties by keeping grandma's dresser; of doing things they once did again, if only they could get interested again. And it could be those kind of dreams aren't American, they're simply human.

That's what industry pros like Adornato are thinking. The business is already firmly established in Australia and Europe, and Adornato has been talking with storage executives about the experience there.

"The executives said over and over again that once people are aware of the product, their habits were indistinguishable from Americans," Adornato reports. "That is, they like to accumulate stuff; they had more stuff than they wanted to keep in their residence; and they had the same inertia about taking it out."

Sonne is bullish on that mother of all markets, China. "One of the developers in China told me the idea of self-storage works everywhere, because people aren't that different." While it might take time to introduce the concept of storage to Chinese consumers, Sonne says, "once it gets in the psyche of people . . . it sort of becomes part of their life."

That means on my next trip to Beijing I might be able to glimpse two Forbidden Cities. The ancient one, full of treasures of jade and calligraphy and hand-wrought bronze, is a museum now, open to the public. But the brand new storage palace, full of magazines and junky bed frames—or the Chinese equivalent—will be walled off and secret. I wonder what dreams will lie in state there.

11

The U.S. Needs to Embrace Sustainability, Not Consumption

Irene A. Quesnot

Irene A. Quesnot works as a minister at St. Mary's University in San Antonio, Texas.

Americans have been infatuated with consumerism for decades, but the recent economic recession has taught many people to tighten their belts and cut down on waste. The nation should use this time to promote sustainability—the concept that all people must use only the resources they need so that society and the planet do not deteriorate from overconsumption. Sustainability projects would encourage industry to limit pollution that affects climate change; it would also compel federal and local government to fund mass transit to lower auto emissions. More significantly, sustainability would impact households, enticing families to cut energy expenditures, buy foods locally, and reduce their overall carbon footprint. The recession has shown Americans that a consumerist lifestyle cannot be maintained indefinitely, so now is the time to prove that everyone can embrace the value of sustainable living.

Going green is not a fad. It's necessary for the continued existence of life on this planet. Despite reputable scientific warnings of inevitable and irreversible damage, depletion persists. Perhaps we don't know enough about what we can do, or we don't care enough.

Irene A. Quesnot, "From Consumption to Sustainability," *National Catholic Reporter*, May 5, 2009, pp. 17–21. Copyright © 2009 The National Catholic Reporter Publishing Company, 115 E. Armour Blvd., Kansas City, MO 64111. All rights reserved. Reproduced by permission of *National Catholic Reporter*. www.NCRonline.org.

Shirley Ann Jackson, president of Rensselaer Polytechnic Institute, sums up the next step: "America needs a bold plan that ignites our collective imagination, sparks innovation and creates economic and national security."

In 2007, the International Panel for Climate Change, the world's most authoritative body of climate scientists, released its Fourth Assessment Report suggesting that the tribulations of climate change are due to human activity and calling everyone into an awareness that we need to do more, particularly when those who struggle most because of climate change are those who have the smaller carbon footprint.

How can we as a nation afford to keep ourselves ignorant of the dangers for others that result from our lifestyle? Imagining all the things we would have to change in our daily lives alone makes us pine after old ways. But change is a part of life, perhaps its very essence. Remember life without cell phones or computers? It wasn't so bad.

Seeing the Recession as an Opportunity

There's further evidence for change's necessity. We are in the middle of a deep recession and many fear what this will mean for our country.

But recession, I believe, can be an opportunity to become more devoted to sustainability than to consumption, and more concerned about what we can do for the Earth's health. A nation realizing its interconnection with the rest of life on the planet would live out a more compassionate and just reality. If we willingly adopt such a lifestyle, not seeing it as a step down in economic status, then we make progress in creating a sustainable America.

Our call to action is to ensure the sustainability of our country while we still can. Part of this action would appeal to economic and national security and involve, for example, federal investment in financing start-up companies, revisiting the hodgepodge system of power transmission regulations, and creating inter-operable standards for smart energy grids. It might also involve offering scholarships to those who focus not only on the relation between ecology and economics but also attempt to create new sustainable technologies for the future.

Recession, I believe, can be an opportunity to become more devoted to sustainability than to consumption.

Attention would have to be paid to the current "cap and trade" system that steadily reduces pollution by having its emitters trade among themselves. Perhaps we can turn to a "cap and dividend" system in which revenues generated from the auctioning of permits are given to households, not to industries.

You then gain if you conserve and lose if you guzzle energy. Revenue comes in the form of equally distributed dividends. This would potentially save the average family $1,160 for a 15 percent cut in emissions, according to the Congressional Budget Office. This system would make it possible to find ecological security in the middle of economic crisis.

Enticing Americans to Go Green

The goal for creating a sustainable United States is centered on the common good and justice for humanity and the Earth itself. Concretely, however, the goal has to focus also on clean energy technology aimed at curbing climate change. Much of this would require that bold ethical imagination.

While taking the bus or local subway system to work instead of driving seems like a legitimate expectation, many people still live in urban sprawl where the walk to the nearest bus stop is over a mile away, and the number of transfers would be a nuisance. Though it may seem excessive to some to transfer to compact fluorescent bulbs to cut on energy usage, doing this can save a person over $120 a year.

Americans would be more likely to practice compassion for the common good if they knew what they would gain from it in the short run.

The goal for creating a sustainable United States is centered on the common good and justice for humanity and the Earth itself.

Cass Sunstein and Richard Thaler's recent book *Nudge: Improving Decisions About Health, Wealth, and Happiness* outlines three principles for bringing about a smaller national carbon footprint.

First, make costs visible. Let people know how much their use of energy is costing them. In trial programs featuring a tabletop ambient orb (a wireless ball that corresponds with the power grid) that glowed red in peak demand periods and green during low periods, homeowners reduced their consumption by 40 percent.

Second, enlist social norms such as neighborly competition by informing homeowners in their bill statements how their energy use compares to people in the neighborhood living in similarly sized houses.

Third, make change simple. Waking up two hours earlier every morning to trek out to the nearest bus stop? It's not practical, but installing a switch in your house that cuts off electricity to all nonessential appliances as you leave the house every morning is easy.

Making Small Changes Has a Big Impact

In this recession, we find ourselves relinquishing our regular occasions of going out to eat. Many families and individuals have decided meals at home are the best option. The price of food, including fresh fruits, vegetables and meats, has skyrocketed. The amount of fuel burned in shipping the fruits and vegetables contributes to a larger carbon footprint and higher costs.

Meat is also regarded as unsustainable since high levels of methane released in factory farming are a leading cause of climate change. Our future in sustainable living would require small changes in each citizen's shopping habits and dietary desires to promote sustainable agriculture and eating. For instance, by eliminating or limiting meats, processed and out-of-season foods in the daily menu, and adding local foods, we improve our health and save money. And it's easy.

Our future in sustainable living would require small changes in each citizen's shopping habits and dietary desires to promote sustainable agriculture and eating.

An extra incentive is that the foods sold at local farmers' markets are raised organically, which not only combats climate change but also diminishes the degradation of life forms and improves the health of workers.

In the midst of recession, we find ourselves stripping away pieces of our lifestyle just to get by. For many this is an uncomfortable reality, but I have hope that what we learn in the art of simplicity in these months or years to come will transform American values of consumption into the values of a sustainable culture by collectively supporting each other in bold imaginings. By implication, this does not harm the Earth, does not pollute our rivers and ocean, and does not lead to the stripping of human dignity for people here or abroad.

Isn't that what our Christian call demands?

12

Sustainability Is a Myth

Peter Goodchild

Peter Goodchild has written several articles on the unsustainability of oil production for various Internet news outlets. He is also a student of Native American culture and the author of Survival Skills of the North American Indians.

Sustainability is a myth. Unrestrained population growth will tax the planet's resources in the coming century, and both food and energy stocks will no longer be able to support humanity. Current attempts to delay the inevitable will never be able to meet the power and resource demands of an exploding population. Thus, the only course left is to determine how to survive the eventual collapse of this culture of overconsumption.

One often hears of the need for "sustainability," and of plans to re-engineer human society in some manner that will enable the production of goods, and the consumption of resources, to extend more or less eternally into the future. Civilization will thereby, we are told, become both more pleasant and more equitable, and the planet itself—land, sea, and sky—will no longer be traumatized by the presence of humans. But those who believe in such sustainability might wish to consider whether such an ideal state is possible.

It is a well-known fact that the human race is in big trouble with overpopulation and with excessive consumption of resources. These two problems reinforce one another; they are synergistic. The message has been around for several years.

Peter Goodchild, "Peak Oil and the Myth of Sustainability," Countercurrents.org, September 6, 2006. Reproduced by permission of the author.

In 1970, for example, Paul and Anne Ehrlich published *Population Resources Environment*. In 1972, Donella H. Meadows et al. published a book entitled *The Limits to Growth* (and there is a later edition called *Limits to Growth: The 30-Year Update*).

Population Growth Demands More Resources

The population of the earth in 1950 was less than three billion. In the year 2000 it was six billion. What it will be in the future is not certain, but a fairly good estimate is that it will be about eight billion by the year 2030. That figure could be off by a billion or so either way, but that would not make much difference. The fact remains that the human population will be doubling again in the near future—unless, of course, something kills us off in the meantime; nearly half the population of England was wiped out by bubonic plague in the fourteenth century.

The peak of oil production will probably be sometime early in the twenty-first century.

Nor can we count on a leveling-off: a slowing of population growth usually occurs in countries that have first become industrialized, and today's overcrowded countries have neither the money nor the political power to become industrialized.

Right now the world is using about thirty billion barrels of oil per year. But the oil is going to run out. The peak of oil production will probably be sometime early in the twenty-first century. (We may have even-passed the peak late in the previous century, although it's hard to tell.) After that point, oil production will rapidly decline. But the demand for oil will not decline. The population, as noted, is still climbing. And contrary to popular belief, computers and other high-tech marvels are not creating a world in which "information will replace transportation." The sales of oil have not decreased with the advent of the "age of information." So—in terms of oil alone, there is a serious problem of resource depletion.

The Fixes Will Fail

Incidentally, "alternative energy" doesn't work. As John Gever et al. explain in *Beyond Oil*, it is physically impossible to use windmills etc. to produce the same amount of energy that we are now getting from thirty billion barrels of oil. "Alternative energy" will never be able to produce more than the tiniest fraction of that amount.

Roughly half the people in the world are either undernourished or malnourished, but agriculture presents one of the worst resource problems. Topsoil is being depleted everywhere. And there is simply no more land available for increased agriculture, unless one considers marginal land that can only be used with expensive high-tech methods of irrigation or perhaps desalination; projects of this sort obviously cannot last long.

One can debate some of the above numbers, but even if we shift them up or down by fifty percent, the general effect is still the same. It is just not possible for the planet Earth to handle "the human condition," nor is there any way of improving those numbers in any significant way. And that's the bottom line. The numbers cannot be changed. The present numbers are just not "sustainable."

Topsoil is being depleted everywhere. And there is simply no more land available for increased agriculture.

Surviving the Fall of an Empire

If all of the above is true, then there is no point in talking about "sustainability." What will happen, in fact, is not sustainability but *disaster*. The future will be one in which the reciprocal effects of overpopulation, resource-consumption, and environmental destruction reach a cataclysmic maximum, resulting in a massive die-off of the human species. There may be survivors, but there will not be many. All talk of sustainability is just fashionable chitchat. The word has use mainly as filler for political speeches. It always sounds good when politicians talk about "sustainable development," when what they really mean is "business-as-usual but with a little ecological whitewash." "Sustainable development" is an oxymoron. If the human race is on a collision course with the three above-mentioned problems, and if there is no way of averting disaster, then there is no point in talking about how to deal with that disaster. It would be far more practical, far more useful, to say: "Okay, disaster is inevitable. What do we do after that?"

The ancient Roman world went through very much the same stages as our own. While Rome was a republic, not an empire, the Roman people adhered to the four virtues of prudence, fortitude, temperance, and justice. But the Roman world became bigger and bigger. There were conflicts between the rich and the poor. There was a serious unemployment problem created by the fact that slave labor was replacing that of free men and women. The army became so large that it was hard to find the money to maintain it, and the use of foreign mercenaries created further problems. Farmland became less productive, and more food had to be imported. The machinery of politics and economics began to break down. The fairly democratic methods of the republic were no longer adequate for a world that stretched from Britain to Egypt, and the emperors took over. After Augustus, however, most of the leaders were both incompetent and corrupt. The Goths sacked Rome in A.D. 410. The Empire was crumbling. The cities and main roads were finally abandoned, since they no longer served a purpose. For the average person, the late Roman world consisted of the village and its surrounding fields.

If we have already established the premise that "the human race faces unsolvable problems," the answer is not to waste further amounts of time and energy in asking whether those problems exist. The best response is to find ways to survive within that problematic world.

Organizations to Contact

The editors have compiled the following list of organizations concerned with the issues debated in this book. The descriptions are derived from materials provided by the organizations. All have publications or information available for interested readers. The list was compiled on the date of publication of the present volume; the information provided here may change. Be aware that many organizations take several weeks or longer to respond to inquiries, so allow as much time as possible.

American Council on Renewable Energy (ACORE)
1600 K St. NW, Suite 700, Washington, DC   20006
(202) 393-0001 • fax: (202) 393-0606
e-mail: info@acore.org
Web site: www.acore.org

ACORE, a nonprofit membership organization, speaks as a central voice for alternative energy sources, such as solar, wind, and biofuel, and works to promote the widespread adoption of these renewable energy sources. Concerned that American energy consumption continues to increase to unsustainable levels, the organization seeks to influence energy policy through its outreach programs, research and publications, and the fostering of communication between industry, media, and government. Annual reports evaluating the status of alternative energy in the United States as well as transcripts of speeches given by organization members can be accessed on the ACORE Web site.

Cato Institute
1000 Massachusetts Ave. NW, Washington, DC   20001-5403
(202) 842-0200 • fax: (202) 842-3490
Web site: www.cato.org

The Cato Institute is a libertarian public policy organization that advocates for limited government, a free market economy, and individual liberty and peace in its policymaking. The institute favors a consumption-based income tax but also stresses the benefits of consumerism. Articles written by institute scholars concerning American consumption include "Sweatshops and Socially Responsible Consumption," "Simplifying Federal Taxes: The Advantages of Consumption-Based Taxation," and "Consumption Versus Income." These articles and others can be accessed on the Cato Institute Web site along with archival copies of the *Cato Journal*, the *Cato Policy Report*, and others.

Center for Economic and Policy Research (CEPR)

1611 Connecticut Ave. NW, Suite 400, Washington, DC 20009
(202) 293-5380 • fax: (202) 588-1356
e-mail: cepr@cepr.net
Web site: www.cepr.net

CEPR is an economic and public policy think-tank that facilitates research on economic and social issues and presents the findings in an easily comprehensible manner to increase the general American public's understanding of the government and democracy. With regard to the economic growth of the country, CEPR has advanced many explanations concerning the economic crisis and recovery, with American consumption being one cause. Detailed reports about the role of consumerism in America can be read on the CEPR Web site.

Economic Policy Institute (EPI)

1333 H St. NW, Suite 300, East Tower
Washington, DC 20005-4707
(202) 775-8810 • fax: (202) 775-0819
e-mail: epi@epi.org
Web site: www.epi.org

EPI is a nonprofit, economic policy research organization seeking to highlight the impact of current economic policies on low- and middle-income American workers and their families. Through its research, publications, and close work with policymakers, EPI seeks to ensure that the voice of working class America is heard. EPI has published numerous reports in recent years showing the harms of increased economic consumption in the United States, including "As Consumption Goes, So Goes the American Economy" and "Consumption Grows at the Expense of Saving." Every two years, it publishes the *State of Working America,* providing current information on the conditions of working class America.

Greenpeace

702 H St. NW, Washington, DC   20001
(800) 326-0959
e-mail: info@wdc.greenpeace.org
Web site: www.greenpeace.org

Founded in 1971, Greenpeace is an environmental organization that works to protect nature worldwide by engaging in non-violent confrontation in order to raise awareness about the destruction of the planet. Greenpeace contends that American consumption of the planet's resources is a threat to the country and the international community, and is a major factor contributing to global warming. Information about U.S. consumption can be found in reports and factsheets on the Greenpeace Web site along with information about alternative energy solutions.

Heritage Foundation

214 Massachusetts Ave. NE, Washington, DC   20002-4999
(202) 546-4400 • fax: (202) 546-8328
e-mail: info@heritage.org
Web site: www.heritage.org

The Heritage Foundation is a conservative research and educational institute that promotes policies in accordance with conservative ideals, such as free enterprise, limited government, individual freedom, traditional American values, and a strong national defense. With regards to consumption, the organization's research encompasses both the economic and environmental fields. The foundation is critical of cap and trade legislation aimed at reducing energy consumption and argues that the current tax code encourages consumption and discourages saving. Articles elucidating these views can be found on the organization's Web site.

Institute for Energy Research (IER)

1100 H St. NW, Suite 400, Washington, DC   20005
(202) 621-2950 • fax: (202) 637-2420
Web site: www.instituteforenergyresearch.org

A nonprofit organization dedicated to the study of energy sources, IER believes that a free market approach to energy production, research, and development will best ensure the adoption of sustainable energy sources. The institute sees government intervention into the energy sector to be a hindrance to the implementation of new energy sources. The IER Web site provides fact sheets and graphs charting U.S. energy consumption by source and sector, as well as information about the most efficient methods to ensure the continued level of energy production necessary to drive the U.S. economy.

Institute for Policy Studies (IPS)

1112 16th St. NW, Suite 600, Washington, DC   20036
(202) 234-9382 • fax: (202) 387-7915
e-mail: info@ips-dc.org
Web site: www.ips-dc.org

Originally an anti-war, civil rights organization, IPS has focused its attention most recently on international peace and justice movements. In addition to its global focus, scholars at IPS also address the problems faced by the middle class in America and have addressed the role of consumption in matters of the economy, environment, and energy-related issues. Articles such as "The Frankenstein Alliance" and "The Commodities Bubble" deal with consumption and its national and global impacts. The IPS Web site provides access to these articles and others concerning the influence of American consumption.

New America Foundation

1899 L St. NW, Suite 400, Washington, DC   20036
(202) 986-2700 • fax: (202) 986-3696
Web site: www.newamerica.net

A non-partisan, nonprofit public policy organization, the New America Foundation empowers people to pursue new solutions to the problems faced in the United States today by focusing on the issues associated with the twenty-first century information-age economy. Specifically, the organization emphasizes the significance of such matters as unemployment, financial imbalances, and increasing inequality. New America has proposed a consumption tax to make tax policy fairer for more American families in the policy paper "Tax Consumption, Not Work." The foundation has also highlighted the negative impact of American consumer culture in the policy paper "America's Consumption Trap." These articles and others can be found on the organization's Web site.

Union of Concerned Scientists (UCS)

2 Brattle Sq., Cambridge, MA   02238-9105
(617) 547-5552 • fax: (617) 864-9405
Web site: www.ucsusa.org

UCS conducts independent scientific research to find solutions to the most pressing environmental and planetary safety concerns and then offers policy recommendations to ensure the implementation of necessary guidelines. The organization has published numerous reports detailing plans to curb U.S. consumption of gasoline, energy, and other sources that contribute to global warming. These plans include the use of hybrid vehicles as well as alternative energy sources; however, UCS opposes the use of nuclear power as a source of energy. Reports detailing these plans and analysis of alternative energy sources can be read on the UCS Web site.

U.S. Department of Energy (DOE)

1000 Independence Ave. SW, Washington, DC   20585
(202) 586-5000 • fax: (202) 586-4403
Web site: www.energy.gov

The DOE mission consists of a three-pronged approach to energy in the United States, including assurance of national economic energy security for the country, support for technological and scientific advances necessary to achieving this goal, and cleaning up the remains of the country's nuclear weapons complex that are potentially damaging to the environment. The department conducts extensive research on climate change, alternative energy supplies, and energy consumption in the United States with fact sheets and reports available on the DOE Web site.

Bibliography

Books

Zygmunt Bauman *Consuming Life*. Malden, MA: Polity, 2007.

John de Graaf, *Affluenza: The All-Consuming* David Wann, and *Epidemic*. San Francisco: Thomas Naylor Berrett-Koehler, 2005.

Andres R. *The Sustainability Revolution: Portrait* Edwards *of a Paradigm Shift*. Gabriola Island, BC, Canada: New Society, 2005.

Charles R. Geisst *Collateral Damaged: The Marketing of Consumer Debt to America*. New York: Bloomberg, 2009.

Paul Hawken, *Natural Capitalism: Creating the Next* Amory Lovins, *Industrial Revolution*. New York: and L. Hunter Little Brown, 1999. Lovins

Gay Hawkins *The Ethics of Waste: How We Relate to Rubbish*. Lanham, MD: Rowman & Littlefield, 2005.

Richard Heinberg *Peak Everything: Waking Up to the Century of Declines*. Gabriola Island, BC, Canada: New Society, 2007.

Tim Kasser *The High Price of Materialism*. Cambridge, MA: MIT Press, 2003.

David Kessler
The End of Overeating: Taking Control of the Insatiable American Appetite. New York: Rodale, 2009.

Annie Leonard
The Story of Stuff: How Our Obsession with Stuff Is Trashing the Planet, Our Communities, and Our Health—and a Vision for Change. New York: Free Press, 2010.

Conrad Lodziak
The Myth of Consumerism. Sterling, VA: Pluto, 2002.

Robert D. Manning
Credit Card Nation: The Consequences of America's Addiction to Credit. New York: Basic, 2001.

Steven Milloy
Green Hell: How Environmentalists Plan to Control Your Life and What You Can Do to Stop Them. Washington, DC: Regnery, 2009.

Michael C. Ruppert
Confronting Collapse: The Crisis of Energy and Money in a Post Peak Oil World. White River Junction, VT: Chelsea Green, 2009.

Ian Rutledge
Addicted to Oil: America's Relentless Drive for Energy Security. New York: Palgrave Macmillan, 2006.

Eric Schlosser
Fast Food Nation. New York: Harper Perennial, 2005.

Juliet B. Schor
The Overspent American: Why We Want What We Don't Need. New York: Harper Perennial, 1999.

Teresa A. Sullivan, Elizabeth Warren, and Jay Westbrook — *The Fragile Middle Class: Americans in Debt*. New Haven, CT: Yale University Press, 2001.

Elizabeth Warren and Amelia Warren Tyagi — *The Two-Income Trap: Why Middle-Class Parents Are Going Broke*. New York: Basic, 2003.

Austin Williams — *The Enemies of Progress: The Dangers of Sustainability*. Charlottesville, VA: Societas, 2008.

Periodicals

Lisa Bannon and Bob Davis — "Spendthrift to Penny Pincher: A Vision of the New Consumer," *Wall Street Journal*, December 17, 2009.

Benjamin R. Barber — "Shrunken Sovereign: Consumerism, Globalism, and American Emptiness," *World Affairs*, Spring 2008.

Robert Barkin — "Sustainonomics," *American City & County*, November 2009.

Tom Bethell — "Has Oil Peaked? Maybe Not," *American Spectator*, October 2008.

David Brooks — "The Next Culture War," *New York Times*, September 29, 2009.

John Carey — "The Biofuel Bubble," *Business Week*, April 27, 2009.

Sophie Chen — "Green with Status Envy," *Psychology Today*, September/October 2009.

Diane Cole "It's Never Too Early to Conserve," *U.S. News & World Report*, April 2009.

Elizabeth Fenner "Too Much Stuff," *Real Simple*, April 2008.

Daniel Gross "Credit Is Dead. Long Live Cash!" *Newsweek*, April 5, 2010.

Alice Aspen March "Wanting and Having Too Much Stuff Can Both Kill or Cure Us!" *American Chronicle*, December 4, 2008.

Kara Nesvig "For Many, Happiness Is a Warm Credit Card," *Star Tribune* (Minneapolis-St. Paul), February 12, 2009.

Richard Stengel "The Responsibility Revolution," *Time*, September 21, 2009.

Erik Stokstad "Americans' Eating Habits More Wasteful Than Ever," *Science Now*, November 25, 2009.

Elizabeth Svoboda "Closet Cases: Hard Times Can Awaken the Hoarder Within," *Psychology Today*, January–February 2009.

Spencer Swartz "World Need for Oil Expected to Ease," *Wall Street Journal*, November 4, 2009.

John Tierney "Use Energy, Get Rich and Save the Planet," *New York Times*, April 21, 2009.

Jim Tillotson   "Americans' Food Shopping in
                       Today's Lousy Economy," *Nutrition
                       Today*, July/August 2009.

Joseph B. White   "Eyes on the Road: What the U.S.
                       Should Do to Cut Oil Consumption,"
                       Wall Street Journal, September 16,
                       2008.

Index

Especially for

....

With love from

....

May you always know who you are in Christ!

For my nieces and nephews:
I pray you will build your life on the foundation
of who God is and what He says about you!
—Dorena

To my parents, Edgar and Perla, and my
husband, William, thank you for believing in my
dreams as if they were yours.
—Dana

I Know Who I Am

Text copyright © 2023 by Dorena Williamson

Cover art and interior illustrations copyright © 2023 by Dana SanMar

All rights reserved.

Published in the United States by WaterBrook, an imprint of Random House, a division of Penguin Random House LLC.

WaterBrook® and its deer colophon are registered trademarks of Penguin Random House LLC.

ISBN 978-0-593-23442-6

Ebook ISBN 978-0-593-23443-3

The Library of Congress catalog record is available at https://lccn.loc.gov/2021048494.

Printed in China

waterbrookmultnomah.com

10 9 8 7 6 5 4 3 2 1

First Edition

Book and cover design by Hannah Hunt and Sonia Persad

Special Sales Most WaterBrook books are available at special quantity discounts when purchased in bulk by corporations, organizations, and special-interest groups. Custom imprinting or excerpting can also be done to fit special needs. For information, please email specialmarketscms@penguinrandomhouse.com.

I KNOW WHO I AM

written by
DORENA WILLIAMSON

WATERBROOK

illustrated by
DANA SANMAR

Look around and you'll see reflections of God's **beauty** and His **truth** about me!

I am beautifully made

and crowned with

glory and strength.

I am filled with God's power.

His Spirit flows through me like a stream of living, moving water!

I am a **precious seed**,
planted in rich soil—
watch me grow!

I am **not afraid,**
for the Lord is **always** with me!

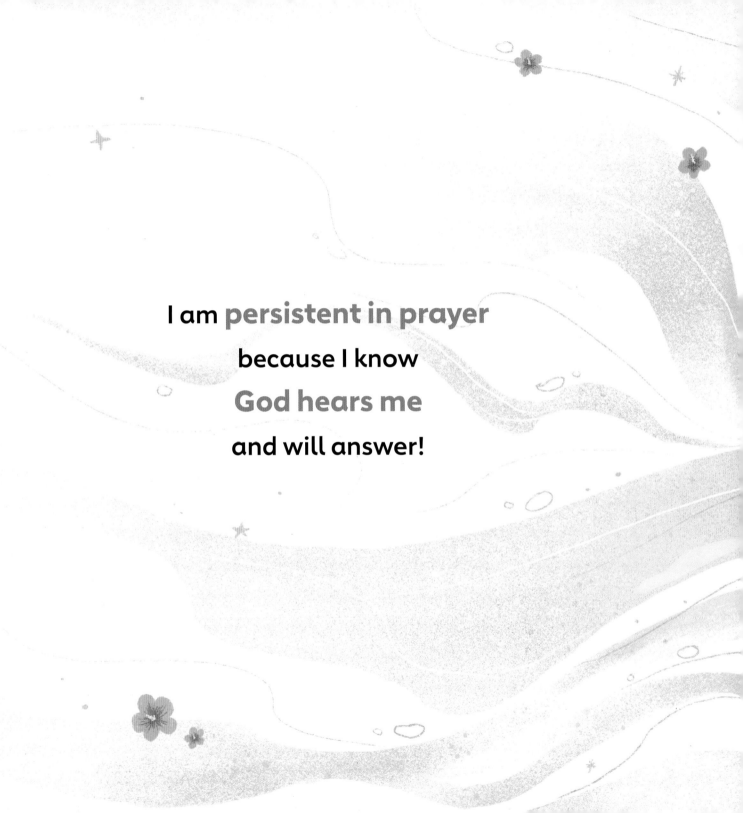

I am **persistent in prayer**
because I know
God hears me
and will answer!

I am full of **God's wisdom.**

His Word is a **treasure**
worth more than silver
and gold.

I have **hope** and a **future** because
God has special plans for me.

I am waiting on God
and trusting that
He will give me strength.

I am **building my life** on Jesus,
the solid rock.

I will **stand firm** through the storms!

I know God will always
take care of me.

He provides
everything I need.

I am **satisfied** because

every good thing comes from
God's hand—He fills me up!

I am more **valuable** to God than all the birds in the sky!

I know I am **great** in God's kingdom!

I am **created** by God and am **fully known** and **loved** by Him. I know who God says I am!

Do you?

Dear friends,

I hope your heart is full after taking in the pages of this story! God's truth is valuable, eternal, and beneficial to us all, and my prayer is that kids will hold on to the precious promises found in His Word. With each reading of *I Know Who I Am*, my hope is that these affirmations sink into the hearts and minds of children of all ages. I want them to believe in these affirmations and declare them over themselves—and their friends as well!

Each spread in this book celebrates a different country and reminds us that people all over the world bear God's light and love.

It was important to have native voices affirm the depictions of their countries of origin, so I want to thank my friends from Haiti, New Zealand, Columbia, the United States, South Korea, India, Rwanda, Mexico, the Philippines, Nigeria, Spain, Romania, Brazil, and Egypt for offering feedback on the illustrations.

Here's to lifting up a generation strengthened by God's truth and assured of His great love!

Derena